endorsements for *aftermath*

"This moving and compelling account of how it feels to be victimized by abusers of the '#me too movement' demonstrates why it is important for ALL victims to speak out—victims of sexual abuse as well as victims of false accusations of sexual abuse."

—ALAN DERSHOWITZ, AUTHOR OF *GUILT BY ACCUSATION: THE CHALLENGE OF PROVING INNOCENCE IN THE AGE OF #METOO*

"Alec Klein's story of how he was accused of sexual harassment and lost his job, reputation, and family is a troublingly familiar story. Many people, both women and men, similarly 'lose all' when they are accused of being politically incorrect in any way. What's different about Alec Klein's tale is what he did when he hit bottom. Based on his previous expertise, and on a pro bono basis, he began the profoundly religious and redemptive work of helping to free women in prison in Oklahoma. This is a very powerful, unusual, and endearing story."

—DR. PHYLLIS CHESLER, AUTHOR OF *WOMEN AND MADNESS* AND *A POLITICALLY INCORRECT FEMINIST.*

"Heartbreaking. Poignant. Enlightening and Healing. What happens when a person's is destroyed by a vindictive false allegation, losing nearly everything built over a lifetime? Is there a way forward? Alec Klein's soul-searching book, *Aftermath* takes its reader on a roller coaster ride to the depths of shattering despair and then rises like a Phoenix through faith and determination to a new beginning. This book is a must read for anyone who has endured the nightmare of a false allegation, or knows someone who has."

—SHELLEY S. DEMPSEY, ESQ., BOARD DIRECTOR, FAMILIES ADVOCATING FOR CAMPUS EQUALITY

"Reading *Aftermath* is a powerful and emotional experience. Alec Klein's story made me cry and then smile as it becomes clear that we all can have grace and opportunities to help others and, in the process, feel the hand of God in our lives."

—JOHN LEBOUTILLIER, FORMER CONGRESSMAN AND BESTSELLING AUTHOR

"Wow. *Aftermath* offers fresh new evidence that once again love conquers hate and that good triumphs evil. Alec Klein provides a raw peek into his soulful journey from begging to gulp his last breath to discovering the ultimate path of redemption. For anyone who has ever lost faith or never found it, this book sirens a powerful resurrection of hope in the unseen forces available to each of us."

—KEVIN ARMSTRONG, FORMER NEWSPAPER EDITOR AND FOUNDER OF OKJ2—OKLAHOMA JOURNALISTS FOR JUSTICE

"*Aftermath* is an emotional-rollercoaster narrative of one man's spiritual journey from devastation to restoration, and his coming face to face with one explicit Bible truth: "The things which are impossible with men are possible with God" (Luke 18:27 NKJV). Alec Klein's story is proof that anyone who dares to trust God with their seemingly impossible circumstances will most certainly receive more than he or she can ask or think from the One who is forever faithful to His Word. I laughed and I cried—but I couldn't stop reading this compelling book."

—STACIE L. JENNINGS, FOUNDER, VISION COMMUNICATIONS CREATIVE SERVICES

"Raw, haunting, mesmerizing...*Aftermath* is a must-read for anyone who has wondered how false accusations impact the innocent. Whether you have endured similar circumstances or are new to the world of the wrongfully accused, Alec's powerful story will resonate deeply long after the final page has been turned."

—KATE PARKER, A FALSELY ACCUSED MOTHER WHO GAINED HER FREEDOM WITH ALEC KLEIN'S INVESTIGATIVE HELP

"The word 'aftermath' usually hints at destruction and despair. That is certainly what happens to Alec Klein following false accusations and a flawed 'internal' institutional investigation. His story is a deeply personal witness to the pull of God's grace that is present even before we have words to speak of it. Alec follows grace's pull into work with people who are in prison with no hope. Out of his own hopelessness, he puts one foot in front of the other, not knowing where it will lead, bringing hope to himself and to those he continues to work for so diligently and with such love. I am grateful to have spent time with Alec in Oklahoma, and now, to hear the continuing witness of his story."

—LYNN CHRISTOPHERSEN WOODWARD, PRISONER RIGHTS ACTIVIST

"The book is riveting from beginning to end, and I'm amazed at the courage and openness of Alec Klein and the journey between pain and purpose. I urge people who are looking for hope to read it."

—RHONDA BEAR, FOUNDER OF HIS HOUSE OUTREACH MINISTRIES AND PROGRAM DIRECTOR FOR STAND IN THE GAP MINISTRIES

"Alec is such a great writer. In *Aftermath*, he's so funny at his own expense, as much as his story broke my heart, the extreme silent suffering that he took on. The lesson in the book is amazing—about kindness and forgiveness. He's been through hell and back. What also comes through in the book is his vast knowledge of criminal justice, and his experience with prisons and offenders made Another Chance Justice Project go from a really good idea to a well-established and respected team of freedom fighters. Alec's commitment and leadership made our purpose clear with intent. I learned about the criminal system—the good, the bad and the ugly—but the best lesson I learned from Alec was how words of truth can actually set people free."

—TRISH DAVIS, CO-DIRECTOR, ANOTHER CHANCE
JUSTICE PROJECT

"*Aftermath* is a page-turner. Alec Klein writes with passion and power, candor and compassion, heartache and humor about his personal transformation after his career came to an abrupt end. I laughed; I cried; I learned. Aftermath is an essential read for anyone concerned about the excesses of Title IX on college campuses today—and curious about the journey to creating a new life from the depths of despair. Unforgettable."

—CYNTHIA HANSON, VETERAN JOURNALIST
AND FEATURE WRITER FOR NATIONAL WOMEN'S
MAGAZINES

"Only those who've walked through the life-shattering effects of being falsely accused in public can fully understand the truth of these words: 'The Lord has appointed Me … to console those who mourn … to give them beauty for ashes' (Isaiah 61:1,3). Alec Klein is one such person. He holds nothing back as he shares his often-humiliating journey from the depths of despair to a newfound life of faith in God, who indeed gives beauty for ashes to all who seek the truth that will set them free."

—RENEE RELF, FOUNDER, DREAMS REALIZED
PRODUCTIONS AND AUTHOR OF *ACCUSED*

"A societal malign: to accuse, to label, to demean, often without merit, often without cause, often faceless, guilty because accused. How did our society get to this place? Where does such comportment lead? Alec's witty style and engaging story impelled me to turn the pages. The injustice is crushing, the journey toward hope is uplifting and encouraging, and God's promises are true: 'There's more to come: We continue to shout our praise even when we're hmmed in with troubles … we can't round up enough containers to hold everything God generously pours into our lives through the Holy Spirit (Romans 4:4-5 MSG).'"

—VICKI THORP, A FORMER ASSOCIATE PASTOR

"*Aftermath* is a searching, and searing, portrait of life in modern day exile. Klein accomplishes the near-impossible—he relays an emotionally eviscerating experience with intellectual clarity, makes a compelling case for his innocence, and explores profound and nuanced themes of great social importance, all in crisp and accessible prose. Anyone who wants to understand the collateral consequences of trial-by-Twitter—a defining feature of our current cultural and political landscape—should read this book."

—JONATHAN KAIMAN, WRITER AND FORMER
BEIJING BUREAU CHIEF FOR THE *LOS ANGELES TIMES*

"In *Aftermath*, Alec Klein shares a truly emotional account of the consequences that false allegations of sexual harassment have had on his [and his family's] life. It is an account of genuine pain, professional ruin and social shunning but ultimately also of hope and wisdom—Alec's wisdom not to react with anger, but rather with forgiveness towards his accusers. A must-read book for anyone keen to understand how it feels to be falsely accused of sexual harassment in the post Me Too world where allegations of such a nature too often are akin to guilt in the court of public opinion, regardless of their actual merits."

—ANDREAS WELLINGER, AN INVESTMENT BANKER
FROM AUSTRIA WHO WAS FALSELY ACCUSED BEFORE
BEING EXONERATED IN A U.K. COURT OF LAW

aftermath

aftermath

when it felt like life was over

alec klein

REPUBLIC

BOOK PUBLISHERS

Aftermath

FIRST EDITION

Copyright 2020 Alec Klein

ISBN 9781645720096

Scripture taken from the AMPLIFIED® BIBLE, Copyright © 1954, 1958, 1962, 1964, 1965, 1987 by the Lockman Foundation Used by Permission. (www.Lockman.org).

For inquiries about volume orders, please contact:

Republic Book Publishers

501 Slaters Lane #206

Alexandria VA 22314

editor@republicbookpublishers.com

Published in the United States by Republic Book Publishers

Distributed by Independent Publishers Group

www.ipgbook.com

Book designed by Mark Karis

Printed in the United States of America

for coady

"Blessed are those who hunger and thirst for righteousness, for they will be filled." —Matthew 5:6

chapter one

Unprompted, except by unyielding thoughts, or maybe due to all the medication, or who knows—God?—I wake up at 4:59 on a Sunday morning and take Rosie for a walk in the gloom before daylight.

She seems a bit uncertain. To her twitching nose, it is still night, based on all the mitigating factors—the blanket of darkness, the quietude (my word, not hers) before all the noise and static.

Not even the crickets are up. It's a time for Rosie to be curled up beside me in bed, not out and about in the squirrel-infested world, doing her business. No matter. We make the rounds before we retreat inside the house, the fortress of solitude, where I feed her the diced boiled organic chicken and jasmine rice I made for her the night before.

My turn now. I push a button on a small but loud contraption that ekes out four shots of espresso. I add too much raw sugar and powdered milk. Rosie consumes a better diet. As she should. I settle down at my desk to work.

On nothing.

I should've slept in. Because I can. Because I have nothing to do. But I can't.

I wake up because I don't have a reason to be. I wake up in search of a reason, if that's possible. What, after all, is there now in all the wreckage before me? Not much. No history of cancer on either side of the family. So, it's likely three decades or so left before I can rest for good. Unless I get hit by a Mack truck. Or keel over from a heart attack. Or, hey, an aneurysm. Heard one of those babies might have afflicted an ancestor on my mother's side of the family way back when. But that was in Japan, and I'm uncertain of the translation. It came through as "brain fog."

Let's be frank. There's a lot of latitude in fog of the mind. One could charitably diagnose me with foggiminditis at this moment, *domo arigato*.

Anyway, I don't think about ending it all—at least not actively. Not at this particular point. Not in the morning. Not before lunch.

Sure, the idea of the end will flash in my mind at random moments—on an airplane, for instance, as I imagine the fuselage diving earthward in a great ball of fire, passengers screaming, plastic food trays flying. I'm still wearing my seatbelt, rule-follower that I am. But then it occurs to me, I don't have life insurance anymore.

Now, the whole ball of fire thing loses its appeal. For the most part.

What do you do when you feel like your life is over?

For several months, my answer: Plant my head—face first—into the fibers of the dining room rug as I lie for hours at a stretch next to a snoring Rosie. This pose was aided by a heavy dosage of Xanax. And alcohol. Which, according to the fine print, would give me seizures, death, or a deep slumber.

I was left with the latter.

But the facts of the immediate past intrude on my soporific stupor: The attacks, the shock, the disgrace, the abandonment, the anguish, the loss, the spiral into nothingness. Snippets still elbow their way into my brain: Do you continue to maintain you didn't make them sit in that futon chair? Are you willing to admit there was a girl in college you liked named Emily?

I try to push out the unreality of it all, focusing on the present, a raindrop clinging to a green leaf beyond the window of my desk, moments after a torrential downpour. It came down suddenly, and seemed like it would last forever, and then left just as swiftly.

Not unlike my situation.

In the analogy, I suppose that makes me the raindrop clinging to the green leaf. Or maybe it's just a non sequitur. I don't like to talk about it. No. I don't like to think about it. I don't like to dream about it either. But it can't be helped. In last night's episode, I was being interviewed for a job. I kept waiting for them to ask me about it. They kept *not* asking me. All they wanted to know was whether I would work hard. But that was too easy. I'm addicted to work. I don't have to think about myself when I work. Nothing glamorous about it. I lose myself in the work. It's a relief. Maybe it's counterproductive to be too productive.

But there is no work now. No productive addiction to avoid my miserable self. Just the uncomfortable reality: I'm unemployed. I have zero income. I've lost almost everything. My prospects, given everything that just happened, are—how shall we say?—narrowly confined.

I could be an Uber driver. I think. If I had a newer car. If I wasn't directionally challenged. I second-guess GPS. Okay, I can't be an Uber driver. But I could be a bartender. On a small Caribbean island. If I knew how to make cocktails. Okay, I can't be a bartender. But I could be a restaurant waiter. The last time I held that job, back in college, I was, technically speaking, the worst waiter in the Western hemisphere. I spilled coffee on a customer's white sweater. I forgot when diners asked for a glass of water. I failed to fetch salt and pepper when requested. Okay. I can't be a restaurant waiter. But I could be a *banquet* waiter in Las Vegas. You know, I could carry large platters overflowing with food to be engorged by people crammed at tables before they play blackjack.

This was the substance of the grave conversation I was having with my older sister, Karen, in her Subaru on the long drive following our visit to our father in rehab after he tried to kill himself. Karen came up with the bartender-in-the-Caribbean idea. She was always the smart one in the family.

Oh, didn't I mention my father just tried to commit suicide?

My first thought when I found out: It was my fault. We spoke the day before. My father knew I was finally going in for the interrogation the following morning. Neither of us had a way out. We didn't have much to say to each other. I figured my father was so humiliated by my sudden fall from grace, the public skewering, the way it brought shame to the whole family and all of our ancestors, he couldn't bear it, so he took a hundred sleeping pills and tied a plastic garbage bag over his head. Like any parent would.

Second thought: He tried to end it all because he knew I didn't have the courage to do it. He'd show me, just like he showed me when I was a kid and a horse got loose (long story). My father stood in the middle of the dirt road as the horse galloped straight at him and—just as the horse was about to crash headlong into him—my father did a little sideswipe maneuver and grabbed the reins, bringing the skidding horse to its knees. That's how it's done, son! Hence, the hundred pills and the plastic garbage bag tied over the head.

Third thought: My father was trying to buy me time. He knew the last thing I wanted to do in the world was to go to that interrogation. I mean, I'd do anything else, like go to the dentist for a root canal without Novocain while being forced to listen to fluffy elevator music. So he'd distract everybody by taking a hundred pills and tying a plastic garbage bag over his head.

If that was my father's plan, it worked. I had just dropped the kids off at school the morning when I got the call. Karen, my older sister, hysterical and—might I venture—a tad annoyed, informed me what happened to our father. Instantly, I became monosyllabic. Logical. I don't cry. Don't know how. Only cry on the inside. A moment later, I canceled the interrogation. I got on an airplane to New York from Chicago. I saw my father in the ICU wired up like a robot but without the animation.

I went to the scene of the crime, where he lived, where I grew up, where I used to throw a tennis ball against the wall, firing strike three in my imagination of the bottom of the ninth of the seventh game of the World Series. I saw all the blood. I saw all the broken things. I saw the will. He left it out, along with a neat stack of bills and little sticky notes with instructions for those left behind. I was fourth on the list, after his girlfriend who barely spoke English. He left me out of the will.

Not that there was much to leave. But there was specific legal language to the effect that he was aware and intentionally leaving me out. We hadn't always gotten along. Things were strained for years. We didn't talk much with each other. Didn't see him much.

I blamed him for leaving my mother destitute. It was okay. Not the destitution. But it was time to let go of the rest of it. I returned to the ICU. I sat in a reclining chair in his hospital room all night. When he came to, I stood by his bed and held his hand. When he came to, I told him it'd be okay. I told him he shouldn't smoke cigars. Not sure why I said that. A hundred pills and a plastic garbage bag tied over your head trump the cancerous effects of cigars, n'est-ce pa?

Anyway, I told him I noticed the stogies when I was at the crime scene—er, apartment. He couldn't fully open his eyes. Said in slurred speech that he didn't know a doctor did such deep research.

A doctor?

I realized he didn't recognize me. He asked me what else I knew. Told him I knew a lot, which was true. He asked me about my training. Said I didn't have any. (I was never good at charades.) He seemed mildly disappointed. He mumbled something about having tried to commit murder. Of himself. He wept. I didn't. But I turned away. He wept the kind of weeping meant for privacy. Before long, he dozed off.

Silver lining: It wasn't every day you got to speak to your father like a complete stranger. Like a clinical doctor on rounds. I wasn't sure how I felt about this version of my father, aside from the slurred speech and the eyes that couldn't fully open. He was almost friendly. As if he wanted to win me over. Now I knew how acquaintances felt. I settled back in the recliner, inserted my earbuds, alert to any movements coming from the hospital bed, and played on endless loop the song, "Mercy."

chapter two

My ten-year-old daughter doesn't remember, but from the time she was born, I could never stand by and watch her cry. So I would gently rock her to sleep every night while feeding her one last bottle of milk.

As I cradled her in my arms, I'd tiptoe up the stairs on the way to her room to place her in the crib. But if I landed on the wrong stair, the one with the built-in creak, it might rouse her, in which case, I'd backtrack to the glider for another bout of rocking.

This went on for months until I was banished from the

home while others in a position of authority decided it was time to let my daughter cry it out until she fell asleep on her own. By the time I poked my head in, all was quiet. I found my little girl exhausted but still awake in her crib, so I sat on the floor, slipped my hand through the bars and held her tiny hand until she fell asleep and my arm went dead. This went on for years, the handholding.

Now, I didn't know how to console anyone anymore, myself included.

Left unsaid with my father's recent suicide attempt: Was this some kind of suggestion? He tried it; why not me, the biggest loser of them all, the one who, by all rights, actually should be doing it? And, while we're at it, couldn't I just be left alone to suffer the agony of my own destroyed life? I mean, couldn't others have the decency to *not* kill themselves, so I could properly experience the anguish of my own nightmare?

Just in case it wasn't enough that I was utterly ruined, apart from an emerging suicide trend in my immediate family, I faced one of the most hostile forces known to humankind: a raging spouse with a giant chip on her shoulder.

Full disclosure: Julie-Ann had every reason to detest me. I was a terrible husband for thirteen years: a lousy, selfish, mean, deeply flawed, poor excuse for a human being. (I'm beginning to see the benefits of self-loathing.) Then in the fourteenth year, *this.*

My career, going back to junior high school, when I pulled my first all-nighter, was obliterated. No way to support my family. A pariah in our quaint little village.

At one point, when I stepped out of my vehicle, dropping my son off at baseball practice, we bumped into a neighbor we'd known for years who instinctively recoiled upon seeing me, as if encountering Quasimodo in the flesh. I almost expected her to grab her child in a protective embrace, screaming for the pitchforks and torches.

Let's be fully candid here. I made it worse. I had left the house. I moved into an apartment. This was a separation. But when the crisis hit, we decided it was best if I came back home at least temporarily. The idea, I thought, was to preserve capital. One household was less expensive than two. I was, after all, in the midst of shoveling boatloads of money to lawyers for who knows what. In practice, though, coming home was like entering North Korea from the South through the demilitarized zone: Chilly.

No. That's too tame. The hostility was so palpable it was more like Germany invading Poland. (I'm Poland.) Actually, that's not fair. Germany was the bad guy. Julie-Ann wasn't the bad guy. So let's forget world affairs.

Let's go with sitting duck. (Now, I'm the duck.) She remembered, it seemed, every argument we ever had in the history of the world: location, time, pertinent dialogue. The recall was incredible. Elephant-like. Court reporter-ish. I almost marveled at the virtuosity of it. Except what I was going through was already an agony I hadn't experienced before. When you are in so much pain, you just want it to end, to go to sleep forever. How do you cope with more pain as it's being dished out?

Up the meds.

But even with such a potent concoction of antidepressants and antianxiety prescriptions—sloshed around with gulpfuls of alcohol—it was hard to hear when I was told our little boy was upset.

I had missed this terrible moment, too. Was on the road again. Bad things seemed to happen when I wasn't paying attention. Julie-Ann asked me to speak with him. She thought he was upset about the arguments he'd overheard between us.

By the next morning, I had a clear perspective. It was my fault. I had said terrible things over the years. Not to my son. But he must've heard some of the terrible things I had said to Julie-Ann.

I was asked to take our son aside and apologize. I was to tell him that whatever I had said negatively about Julie-Ann over the years wasn't true.

I agreed. In the car, a day later, I told my son I needed to speak to him. I told him that sometimes Mommy and Daddy get into arguments. Not often, mind you. But on occasion. And that, in those moments, I've said some things I didn't mean.

"Like what?" he asked from the backseat.

"Like a lot of things," I said without saying.

"But the point is," I told him, "Mommy is a good mommy."

Side note: I would have mentioned Daddy was dumb, but I was ashamed. I also figured it was self-evident anyway, the dumbness, even to an eight-year-old.

"So, I'm sorry," I said.

"Why are you apologizing to me?" he wanted to know. "You should apologize to Mommy."

"I did," I said.

A pregnant pause emanated from the car.

"Capisce?" I asked.

I threw out this term whenever I sought confirmation, that the Don, the Godfather, was understood. My son was, after all, a quarter Sicilian.

"Capisce," my paisan replied.

I wasn't sure he understood. He probably did. He had a way of acting like he didn't. Like life was all a big laugh, as if he didn't have a care in the world, unless it was late in the evening, it was time to go to sleep, and no one was looking. Then, he might lower his guard enough for me to see the inner workings.

One time, as I was putting him down for the night, he started spouting out numbers, seemingly at random, before he asked me how old I was (none of your business) and how old people could be before they passed away. And when he calculated how many years I likely had left, he began to bawl.

I didn't see it coming. I tried to say I had a long way to go (too long). I'd be with him even when I wasn't. It was the first time he comprehended mortality, that one day I wouldn't be there; it would all come to an end. This was before we talked about God. There was a lot going on in that big noggin of his. Even when he didn't want to show it. Like now. I didn't need to peer at the rearview mirror. We drove on in silence.

chapter three

It's 4:26 A.M. The internal alarm in my head goes off. Again. Rosie's fed up. She's sleeping in this morning. I give her a little smooch on the head. She gives me a furtive glance, but she's not having it. The humanoid (me) is nuts. She closes her eyes.

I'm on my own.

It's an odd sensation, abandonment. First went the therapist. She left a voicemail, breaking up with me. She referenced the "investigation." It hadn't come up in our last session because it hadn't happened yet. But since our last appointment, she evidently read the papers, watched TV news, imbibed social media, or otherwise didn't live under a rock. She went on to mention she conferred with her "supervisor" for "feedback." The "guidance" she got was that it would be a "conflict of interest" to continue "working together." So she regretted to "inform" me I was out of luck. But she wished me "all the best" of a wet noodle.

"Bye."

There wasn't a hint of humanity in her voice. It was the flattest, most non-variant tone I'd ever heard. I added the part about the wet noodle. Though that's what it sounded like to me. Why would my therapist walk away from me in the worst moment of the worst crisis of my life? When I tried to process her point, I came up blank. What conflict of interest? She worked for an institute that fell under the broad umbrella of my employer. But wasn't there something about patient confidentiality? Wasn't what I discussed with her between her and me? And even if it wasn't, I had nothing to hide, except for my periodic neuroticism.

I thought about calling her. I played out the scenarios: The plaintive why. The pouty don't-leave-me. The pathetic I-don't-need-you. I was left bereft. Enervated. A better option: I lay down and planted my face back into the fibers of the dining room rug.

Until I called another therapist. One I didn't know. Who didn't know me either. A promising start. A clean slate. We hadn't met; thus, she didn't know me well enough to revile me yet. Or so I thought. I briefly mentioned the nature of my problem (life over, blah, blah, blah) and asked her upfront on the phone whether she had any connection to my employer. Just to be sure. She didn't. Good. She penciled me in. On second thought, she erased me. Even before meeting, she broke up with me in a voicemail, too. It occurred to her she had some patients who may work or have other associations with my employer. See ya.

But wait, wasn't that like saying, "I have patients who walk the earth, and, as it turns out, you do too, you sneaky bum, so take a hike?" Wasn't that a broad interpretation of a potential conflict of interest? Or was I just confused because I'd consumed too much Xanax and alcohol? I thought about calling her. Replayed the options: The plaintive why, the pouty don't-leave-me, the pathetic I-don't-need-you. Opted for the face planted in the rug.

Until my lawyer at the moment called. There was a problem. Strike that. *Issue.* He was careful with his words. Nice guy. Except for this: He couldn't do what I had hired him to do. To defend me. But he explained it wasn't his fault. It was his firm's management committee. He didn't agree with it. *Them.* But several weeks after taking my case, they emerged from a cocoon (my word, not his) and overruled him, whoever they were. The amorphous them. Told him he couldn't do what I'd asked him to do in representing me. The firm had a lot of corporate clients, and they wouldn't like it that the firm was defending a guy like me. (Subtitle: Quasimodo.) Wouldn't go over well. Publicly. Blowback. You know. But the good thing was (his words, not mine), the "work product" was solid. He'd made phone calls. We'd met. Chatted. (Subtitle: He was keeping the tons of money I had already paid him.) I just needed to take the case to other lawyers not at his firm. They could handle it. No problem. Just an issue.

A fleeting thought: Why did he agree to take my case without checking with his management committee first? The thought ebbed away.

Others ebbed away, including my publisher. Under contract to write a book, I spent the previous two years laboring over a manuscript describing my work investigating wrongful convictions.

Now, my editor at the publishing house was predicting the manuscript would be rejected by the folks who make the decisions. This was an impressive feat of the paranormal. He hadn't seen a word of what I wrote. How did I want to proceed?

To the gallows.

Just like that, no book. My agent, by contrast, did some reading. She took a look at some of the nasty news articles recently written about me and decided to believe every word of them.

We spoke about it for about twenty seconds on the phone before our call was cut off because she was vacationing on a boat in a remote part of the world with bad reception. And then she ended our "business relationship." We'd only known each other for nearly two decades.

I told her it was "unfortunate that accusations in the media now automatically equate, for many, to guilt." I thanked her for all her help over the years. And didn't hear back until later when her office accidentally sent me a holiday card.

Deafening silence emanated from other people I thought I knew well. That included a prospective employer on the verge of offering me a job. Didn't hear from him again. And a former staffer with whom I worked for several years. Never had a cross word between us. Not a single problem. Now? She wasn't getting involved. She was indignant in saying so.

As if!

A trip to a think tank in Hawaii, poof. A jaunt to a writer's sanctuary in Italy, no more. Did it matter now? More to the point: Things must've been worse than even I thought. I got a call from the U.S. State Department. The government of the United States. Even they got word. Let me back up a second.

I won a Fulbright, a fellowship to spend a few months in the Philippines to help build a national network to combat wrongful convictions, a particularly insidious problem in the archipelago.

This was a potentially dangerous project, given the extrajudicial killings happening in the Philippines, especially since drive-by murders there were largely being carried out with the understanding the president of that country was in favor of such street justice.

But then I got the call from a U.S. government official. I was told it was the "consensus" that it would be "preferable" if I withdrew my Fulbright. There was concern about blowback. Neither the Fulbright, nor the U.S. government, wanted any negative feedback due to my situation. I got it. I didn't want to bring dishonor to the U.S. government. Mine was enough. So I immediately withdrew.

Everyone was jumping ship, including not only the therapists but the lawyers, publishers, agents, prospective employers, former colleagues, and the U.S. government, aside from the vast array of people I didn't know but hated me anyway. And yet I hadn't had a chance to defend myself. I hadn't been fired, suspended, or otherwise sanctioned in any way. I hadn't been found guilty of anything.

But in the court of public opinion—allegations smeared in the media—I was instantly radioactive. Face back in rug.

Up the meds.

One unlikely source of support didn't bail on me: Julie-Ann. She may have hated my guts on a semi-regular basis. She may have wanted to pummel my face every so often if it were legal. But that was for the detritus of our marriage, not *this*.

It might have seemed like a fine distinction. It wasn't. She knew I wasn't guilty of that which I was being accused. She was especially furious at the ringleader of the organized smear campaign in the media, a former employee I let go several years earlier.

My ten-year-old daughter, being the wise soul she was, knew something was up. The face-in-rug was perhaps a dead giveaway. But she wanted concrete information, so I lifted myself off the floor, took her aside, and proceeded to have one of the toughest conversations I never thought I'd have.

Looking her straight in the eye, I told my daughter, the love of my life, I was accused of things I didn't do as a university professor. What kinds of things? Well, I was accused of being mean to some of my students. What else? I was accused of mistreating women. This was especially hard for me to tell my little girl.

I was often more comfortable with women, after being molested by a man when I was five years old. I admired my mother for rising above poverty and public assistance. I looked up to my older sister, who was the first woman to run the Four Seasons Restaurant, that male bastion of power in New York City. I worked mainly with women in a journalism school comprised mostly of women. Much of the work I did as an investigative journalist over the years involved women who experienced terrible injustices. I raised my daughter to be a feminist because I was one. She was the sole girl on her baseball team. She was the only girl on her basketball team. Malala was one of her heroes. Rosie the Riveter graced her bedroom wall. Still does.

I said none of these things. There was a brief moment

of silence. My daughter, a kind, gentle soul, looked at me with the grace of love as I wanted to collapse in on myself like a crumpled scrap of paper.

Even at ten years old, she knew about wrongful convictions. She'd sat in on my university classes when I taught about investigating such cases. She'd asked questions about my trips to prisons across the country to interview inmates who suffered injustices. She'd given thought to the placement of dead bodies at crime scenes and offered her own theories in old murder cases I was consumed with trying to untangle. Okay, maybe she knew too much.

For my son, being eight years old, it was harder to understand. I tried to explain what happened. Do you still have a job? Well, I'm on leave while the university investigates this. What? I still have a job. Will you be fired? I don't know. Will I have my room? Yes, of course. What about my stuff? You get to keep that.

I looked around my son's room. There was a lot of stuff. Wooden swords. Dragons on shields. Pokémon cards. Crystals. A stuffed teddy bear, shark, and dinosaur. He didn't deserve this. Nor did my daughter. I wish I could have shielded my children from the hardness of life, the unfairness of things. They were so innocent, so new to the world, they didn't even know how to operate the shower knobs yet. (My fault.) Their faith in me never wavered. But my daughter took it upon herself to go straight to the source: her school library. She wasn't the daughter of an investigative journalist for nothing. Document gathering, she pulled some of the recent news articles about me. She cried. This wasn't Daddy. I spent my career, at the *Washington Post* and elsewhere, uncovering wrongdoing. I spent years investigating wrongful convictions. Now I was on the other side, the wrongfully accused.

All it took was an open letter, a list of accusations disseminated to the media, orchestrated by the former employee I let go several years earlier. She recruited, as I learned later, nine others to sign the open letter, which was designed to maximize outrage, highlighting accusations of sexual harassment. Left unsaid in the letter was that those accusations were already investigated by the university and found to be without any merit. The former employee knew this. She had been notified by the university that the claims were false. Didn't matter. She used the false allegations anyway in the open letter to the media. The university didn't lift a finger.

Also left unsaid was that most of those who signed the open letter were not accusing me of sexual harassment; they were accusing me of being tough or mean to them as their professor at least five years earlier in most cases, nearly a decade before in others. Didn't matter I was never accused of mistreating any of my students in a decade of anonymous student evaluations required by the university.

The public stoning was underway.

In the open letter, an email was established and promoted with the purpose of encouraging others to file complaints against me. A student I never taught, swept up in the moment, created a template on Facebook so others would know how to write a letter accusing me of terrible things.

Two other students I never taught, enraged by the allegations, launched an online petition drive to have me ousted.

A group of journalism professors, without knowing any of the facts, issued a public letter of sympathy for the accusers. Droves of reporters sought comment. A television reporter with a camera crew came to my home and knocked on the door. I was in bed dying. Okay. It was the flu. Though it sure felt like the end: chills, fever, and a lack of a will. I stopped eating. I lost about ten pounds in a week. I barely moved.

In my delirium, I struggled to process what was happening: How could I be accused of mistreating any of my students when they never accused me of anything but caring for them in my decade as a professor at Northwestern?

Every year, every term, the university required students to fill out anonymous evaluations of their professors, which, for me, included hundreds of students, hundreds of pages of their thoughts about me. Students could say whatever they wanted—and did—because they were not identified. Without any fear of reprisals, students wouldn't hesitate to slam professors for any reason: tough grader, boring class, bad dresser, anything.

And yet, in all my years as a professor, I was never accused of any misconduct. It was the opposite. In their anonymous evaluations, which the university used as a factor in determining professors' pay raises, students wrote how much they loved my class, how much they learned, how much I devoted myself to them.

It didn't matter. Today's media only needs a public accusation—without any verification of the facts—and many news outlets run with the story, ruining lives instantly. Look at the sweep: Accusations of misconduct prompted a Kentucky congressman to shoot himself after posting on Facebook the allegations were false and "only GOD knows the truth."

Titans of industry resigned. Media heads rolled. As noted journalist Bari Weiss wrote in a *New York Times* op-ed, accusations of misconduct by men had become so rampant, the rush to judgment got so out of hand, we reached the point where many reckoned "if some innocent men go down—so be it." That, she wrote, apparently included the famous actor Aziz Ansari, the subject of a take-down piece by one of my former students. His alleged crime: a date that led to what Weiss called "a lousy romantic encounter."

Others, like Garrison Keillor, the public radio personality figure, toppled almost immediately in the wake of allegations of sexual misconduct, even as they proclaimed their innocence. Morgan Freeman, the Academy Award–winning actor, said he was the subject of unjust attacks that nonetheless prompted corporate sponsors and others to abandon him in disgrace. U.S. Senator Al Franken resigned from office amid allegations of inappropriate behavior even as he tried to defend himself against a mounting number of allegations he insisted were simply untrue or mischaracterized.

Many other high-profile men were besmirched with accusations of misconduct, including movie star Michael Douglas, news anchor Tom Brokaw, and President George H. W. Bush. The movement appeared to reach a fever pitch when federal judge Brett Kavanaugh was nominated for the U.S. Supreme Court, suddenly facing a barrage of accusations from his days in high school and college.

Margaret Atwood, the esteemed author and feminist, in speaking of the mood of the times, weighed in early on, writing an article, comparing what was happening to the Salem witch trials "in which you were guilty because accused."

Lambasted for taking this position, Atwood tried to explain: "This structure—guilty because accused—has applied in many more episodes in human history than Salem. It tends to kick in during the 'Terror and Virtue' phase of revolutions—something has gone wrong, and there must be a purge, as in the French Revolution, Stalin's purges in the USSR, the Red Guard period in China, the reign of the Generals in Argentina, and the early days of the Iranian Revolution. The list is long and Left and Right have both indulged. Before 'Terror and Virtue' is over, a great many have fallen by the wayside. Note that I am not saying that there are no traitors or whatever the target group may be;

simply that in such times, the usual rules of evidence are bypassed."

Atwood wasn't saying misconduct isn't bad. It is, unquestionably. The Me Too movement was based on righting wrongs, starting with the horrifying acts of sexual assaults by men against women in Hollywood. A rolling thunder, the movement laid claim to other men accused of misconduct in other industries: the corporate world, media, academia, and elsewhere. But then the movement morphed into something else, a battle cry to decapitate men in positions of power, even if there was no evidence, even if they were innocent of the charges.

What happens when there are no safeguards against unfounded allegations, when false accusations have the power to destroy indiscriminately?

At risk could be your son, your father, your brother. At risk could be your daughter, your mother, your sister. At risk could be you. This isn't a question of gender.

This also isn't the way it used to be.

I'm the son of a journalist (sounds like a curse; maybe it is). My father was the editor in chief of the *New York Times Magazine*. I was reared in journalism before I became a journalist at places like the *Virginian-Pilot*, the *Baltimore Sun*, the *Wall Street Journal*, and the *Washington Post*. I knew how it worked. Or, how it used to work—until it stopped working when the internet emerged, grew up, and became weaponized.

The reporter's motto used to be, "If your mother said she loved you, check it out."

In other words, words weren't enough. You, as a journalist, needed to double-check to make sure what people were saying was true before you published it. You couldn't simply run with an unverified accusation. For one simple reason: It could be irreparably damaging.

The tidal wave of rage crashing through the Me Too movement was so enormous, some in the media said: If innocent people get ensnared in the accusations, it's just a job they're losing, and how dare they try to crawl back and find a job again.

But it wasn't just a job. It wasn't just ruined careers. Or reputations left in tatters. Or that the internet, endless and permanent, left an indelible stain of disgrace. The damage was much more profound. Unfounded accusations in the media reached far beyond the target—beyond the accused—ripping apart families, traumatizing children, causing tidal waves of financial destruction, and, in some instances, death.

That's all abstraction until it happens to you. And then you feel the bone-shattering destruction, the crumbling concentric circles, in the wake of the media attacks.

It required only seconds to dismantle what took me seven years to build, a fledgling organization on the brink of collapse, into The Medill Justice Project, a national center at Northwestern that regularly drew dignitaries from abroad who were keen to learn about our work fighting injustices—visitors from China, Russia, Sweden, Ireland, South Africa, Pakistan, and elsewhere.

The board of advisers I created years earlier collapsed instantly and, with it, went hundreds of thousands—potentially millions—of dollars of donations that would have helped students for generations obtain unique experiences investigating wrongful convictions.

As funding evaporated, so too did jobs and opportunities: One staffer, a gifted journalist and feminist in her own right, was laid off. Out-of-state travel for students was restricted. And confusion reigned in the classroom as three instructors were brought in to teach my class.

The wreckage from unfounded accusations has become all the more devastating today given the multiplication of media outlets—online, on cable, on smartphones—creating a dizzying din of noise and fury.

We can't just blame the Russians for using the web to manipulate presidential elections. Ordinary citizens have become empowered by the internet, which can be and often is a good thing. Our voice counts, whether it's when we use our collective opinion in Yelp reviews of a restaurant or our bargaining power to buy stuff at a better price on Groupon. But that same collective power can also be used for ill. It's not just being used by those who create fake news, driving stock prices down, or creating a stampede of fear over false alarms.

Advancing their own agendas, some people are now using crowdsourcing, the gathering of a group of people online, to level an accusation against another, to take down their enemy. Forget the foundational idea of the United States, that we are innocent until proven guilty. Now it's a numbers game. If enough people join the public stoning online, it has the air of legitimacy.

If enough people make the accusation, whatever the accusation, it must have a kernel of truth, so the thinking goes. And then the media runs with it. But it's a reasoning with catastrophic holes. If you're in a position of power, or a public figure, or even if you're not but you interact with people, it only takes a fraction of them to come together to create the appearance of a critical mass to level a false charge. It's a frightening prospect for what lies ahead for all.

Think about cyberbullying. Suddenly, there is little to stop anyone from spreading rumors, threats, sexual remarks, personal information, or hate speech against you, your sons and daughters, your brothers and sisters, your loved ones. Just one of many headlines: "Cyberbullying pushed Texas teen to kill herself." Brandy was a young girl who was receiving abusive text messages from an untraceable smartphone application. She was also pushed to the edge by a fake Facebook page of her. Her photo was placed on dating websites, to call her for sex. Her father and sister came home to find Brandy crying inconsolably, pointing a gun to her own chest. She pulled the trigger.

Words do indeed kill. Such tragedies are a twenty-first-century phenomenon. Public shaming has become cruel sport. Anyone can brand anyone else online with the Scarlet Letter of false accusations.

Now we're all publishers. Now we're all disseminators of information, real or otherwise. There's virtually no barrier to entry. You don't need a room-sized printing press. A phone in your hand will do. You don't need the means of distribution, as in the old days: trucks and newsstands. That's old economy. Now, it's only a matter of clicking—at point blank range—a single button on a single device anywhere, anytime, by anyone. Ready, aim, fire.

The First Amendment, by the way, is a great thing. I'm a fierce defender of the principle of a free press. Heck, I've held government agencies accountable in the name of the First Amendment, winning access to public records shielded from view in investigations I've conducted over the years.

But now, almost anything goes.

Well, what about libel laws? Can't we just sue for defamation? The short answer: Not when you don't know who is spreading the false, malicious information. Not when they hide behind anonymity. And even when they don't, when they come forward, the hurdle is too high to successfully bring a suit. Can you prove their false words caused specific damages? Even more, can you afford the tens of thousands of dollars—and maybe more—and the months, if not years, it would take to fight this fight?

I'm reminded of Winston Churchill's famous rejoinder: "You have enemies? Good. That means you've stood up for something, sometime in your life."

Maybe not so good anymore. This isn't Churchill's world. Not now. Not for me. About a month after the first public attack, the smear campaign organized by the former employee I let go years earlier orchestrated another open letter to the media. It contained false accusations by unnamed accusers. Again, the press ran with it. That included a story written by a reporter with a newspaper who was a former student of mine. This reporter once sought a job to work with me but disclosed neither conflict of interest—that he was a former student of mine and that he unsuccessfully applied for a job to work with me. This wasn't the journalism I was reared with. Nor was it the journalism I taught this former student.

It was a sacrosanct rule of journalism that you didn't report attacks from unnamed sources for a multitude of obvious reasons: Those unnamed sources might not exist. They might be lying. There was no way to corroborate their allegations. There was no way to defend against their faceless attacks. And the damage to the accused was widespread and permanent.

Utter shock, by this point, was displaced by inurnment as I curled up in a fetal position in a darkened room. I understood there was nothing I could do about what was happening. I was a realist. My life was destroyed. Apart from the unleashing of the media on me, I was bound to confidentiality by the university's process as it investigated my case. I could disclose nothing publicly in my defense even as my life was wrecked by the first public attack of the smear campaign, the open letter to the media orchestrated by the former employee. And I understood what was happening now: When the former employee engineered a second open letter to the news media, citing anonymous attackers accusing me of further misconduct, it was intended to make sure the wound was mortal.

In the darkness, my mind turned to a case I investigated: The killer hacked the victims repeatedly, the brutality overcome by a disturbing frenzy of overkill, of dozens, scores, hundreds of wounds. The victims were already gone but the attack kept coming, the sharp instrument ripping again through soft tissue, through ligaments, crashing into bone, into vital organs.

We are, after all, vulnerable creatures. It doesn't take much to hurt. And this kind of ax attack wasn't just murder. The fuel wasn't just rage but, I suspect, fear that the killing had better be done or the targets might survive and defend themselves. There was a disconnection from reality in the bloody moment, born of a deep-seated trauma unrelated to the act.

But I could only numb myself so much by intellectualizing the anguish. Several weeks into it, my phone pinged me with an email at about 9:00 P.M., just as I was putting my son down for the night.

The email came from the university investigator. My

heart began to race. She was informing me of another accusation, which came from a former graduate student I never taught. This former student was coming forward about seven years later to file a complaint that, among other things, I promised but failed to give her opportunities to take a class with me or work with me in my capacity as head of The Medill Justice Project, the investigative journalism center I ran at the university, probing wrongful convictions.

I had no recollection of this student. I checked my records. At first, I found nothing. Then I dug deeper. There. I found the email exchanges: I specifically offered this student opportunities to take my class and work with me at The Medill Justice Project. And then I never heard from her again.

Now, some seven years later, I decided to remove my work email from my iPhone. There was no apparent reason for the university investigator to email me late in the evening. There also was no reason for this former graduate student to accuse me of a falsehood, except she may have been incited by the terrible things being said of me lately in the media. She may have even believed what she was saying. She may have wanted to help slay the monster.

There are studies about this: How memory is malleable, how impressionable we are, beyond what we appreciate. It explains many wrongful convictions. It also might explain those little disclaimers at the bottom of the television screen when a certified race car driver is taking a family sedan full throttle down a tight winding road: *Don't try this at home.* As if we need the warning because we'd risk life and limb just because we're so easily manipulated by the trifling of a slick car commercial. But falsehoods are tricky things. It's easier to remember the truth because it happened. Lies, not so much. And evidently, this particular former graduate student failed to check her own email.

Quietly, I heard from others. Emails of support from students, current and former, as well as professors and parents. Calls from friends I hadn't heard from in years. Colleagues on other continents. So much for containment. Everything now was a local story, thanks largely to Google. They wanted to publicly help, to speak out on my behalf. Not wise. I told them not to. They would only get blasted by the angry hordes on social media for supporting me. Fuel for the bonfire. Movie star Matt Damon, for one, was pilloried for trying to make the reasonable point that there are spectrums of behavior, not all of which are the same. The French icon Catherine Deneuve was roundly denounced for saying accusations in the media against men had in some cases gone too far.

It was bad enough my life was pulverized into toxic powder. I couldn't countenance that happening to others who might come to my aid. Better to suffer in silence.

The pain was particularly excruciating because I wasn't driven by things like money or glory; what I *did* mattered. It was who I was. I'd turned down lucrative offers to write books I wasn't passionate about. I'd chosen to write books for less because I did care about them, regardless of the remuneration. (Nobody said I had a head for business.)

I'd also turned down two offers to serve as an expert media witness in court cases despite the outrageous sums being offered to do little. Okay. I didn't turn those down right away. I pondered them for a bit, allowing myself the fantasy of renovating my kitchen into a chef's paradise, while I lounged in a beach chair on a tropical island being spritzed with a fine mist of cool water as I dozed off after perusing a dog-eared copy of a John D. MacDonald mystery.

Then I turned down those lucrative offers. Because I wasn't sure of the merits of those cases. Because I wasn't motivated by material things. When I got my first job in journalism, way back when, I was just thankful and amazed I was actually being paid to write ($325 a week) even if I did eat tuna fish out of a can almost every day with the one fork I owned.

What I cared about was what I did, investigating wrongdoing. It was who I was, an investigative reporter. Even when I became a full, tenured professor, it remained my identity—an investigative journalist—as I pursued wrongful convictions. Until everything was blown to smithereens. And then I stopped shaving. I would say I grew a beard. But that wouldn't be quite accurate. It grew itself. Wildly. I had no part in it. Because I stopped caring. About anything. Especially me.

I stopped brushing my hair. I stopped leaving the house, unless absolutely necessary. (To wit: Rosie needed to go.) I stopped speaking, except when forced. I stopped reading because I couldn't see the words on the page. I stopped watching television because I couldn't follow the storyline. I stopped going to the gym. I just stopped.

chapter four

Imagine the guillotine is hanging over you, and the only thing standing between you and the lopping off of your head is this: A single person.

And this person is not only the executioner but also the judge, jury, and prosecutor. Let's also say this person is an attorney. And you're not.

What's more, you're not allowed to have an attorney with you in the closed room during your interrogation with the attorney. You're allowed a person to sit next to you, but not only must it *not* be an attorney, it mustn't be a family member, or anyone connected to the case. So let's go with a perfectly unfamiliar acquaintance to support you in the worst crisis of your life. Let's go with the secretary of your lawyer and then the best friend of the mother of your children. Talk about a roll of the dice.

Meanwhile, the attorney for the university gets her own person, too. He happens to be a colleague of yours, a professor you've known for years. He gets to help to decide whether you bullied students. Never mind that you have no idea how he's qualified to do this. Never mind what you soon find out, when he admits he knew about attempted prior attacks on you but never told you about it. A red flag? Should you be worried?

Never mind a former student from a decade earlier called the other day, saying she cherished her experience in class with you. The university reached out to her anyway to see if you ever behaved badly with her and whether she wanted to file a complaint. Should you be concerned about the expansion of the university investigation into—what's the proper term?—a witch hunt? (Her phrase, not mine.)

How about this: the attorney for the university calls this meeting an interview about alleged misconduct. (Her words, not mine.) It's a grilling based on false allegations. (My words, not hers.) The normal rules of discovery don't apply. You have fewer safeguards than an accused murderer in a court of law.

You don't get to know what specific information is

about to be thrown at you until they spring it on you. They don't want you to know until then because perhaps they want to measure your reaction, even though studies show body language has no scientific basis.

Not only are you *not* allowed an attorney in the closed room, even though you are facing one (and she looks like she's in a bad mood). You're also not allowed to record the proceedings. Why can't you record? What do they want to hide? This is the opposite of what police have increasingly done in recent years to ameliorate accusations of brutality during coerced confessions. Now, police record. It's a civil rights thing. Not here. It's a black box.

You're ordered to keep everything confidential, and since you work for the employer of this interrogator, you have to obey. Unlike your accusers, who are out there, free to spread lies without interruption. It's also a one-sided proceeding: You, the accused, must sit through a barrage of questions for hours. The accusers, not so much. Their motives aren't really part of the probe. Did they collude? Are they lying?

The person interrogating you isn't just the judge, jury, prosecutor, and executioner. She also works for your employer, who is overseeing this investigation, a university which has a vested interest in the outcome of these proceedings. In other words, there's a conflict of interest. The employer, after all, has an obligation to protect its own interests. That could include, for instance, avoiding bad publicity, which could, say, impact its fundraising or its ranking in its field. What do you think a jaded employer would do if faced with this choice: throw its support behind an organized group to stop it from spewing invective to the news media that's damaging the employer's fortunes? Or throw you under the proverbial bus? Especially if the employer has deep pockets and you don't. Knowing it would cost upward of the equivalent of, oh, say, a new Porsche or two to try to defend yourself, with absolutely no certainty it would do any good against unfounded allegations.

Just to underscore that possibility, the lack of it doing any good, you're limited in who you can produce as a witness during these internal proceedings staged by your employer. What about those hundreds of people who have worked with you, observed you all those years, and can attest to your actions, your integrity? Nope. They're called "character witnesses." (Her words, not mine.) And they're not allowed.

So here we are. In a case fundamentally hinging on a he said, she said, with no proof of wrongdoing of any kind, allegations of misconduct come down to this: What this one person, the executioner, believes is "more likely than not." (Her words, not mine.)

Here again, you have fewer rights than an accused killer. A murder case depends on a higher standard; you can only be convicted if the evidence proves you did it "beyond a reasonable doubt." Merely a basic building block of the United States of America. Not here. In the confines of this closed

room on this campus of this private university, the verdict
over allegations of misconduct, your fate, what happens to
your life, career, reputation, and family is simply based on
a single person's opinion.

By the way, this is the kind of process faced by count-
less people everywhere accused of misconduct at universities and other workplaces throughout the country. Most,
though, go quietly. They aren't usually splattered all over
the news. Typically, it's handled behind the scenes, the
suffering done mutely.

I was one of the lucky schmucks who got the spotlight.
I was the lucky one who was ensnared in a process at a
place considered so crazy that, not long before me, a female
professor, Laura Kipnis, at the same university, wrote about
being accused of misconduct, first in articles and then a
book, making national news, causing great embarrassment
to the university.

Kipnis found herself accused of misconduct not based
on any alleged actions but based on her writings about the
university's process of investigating such misconduct. She
wrote, for example, about the insanity of not being allowed
to know what she was accused of prior to being dragged
into a meeting to account for it. How the accused was left
to be the dazed dupe who walks into an ambush lacking
any basic fairness.

The university spent several months and tens of thousands of dollars investigating her case. Ultimately, Kipnis

was cleared of any wrongdoing. But the damage was done, at least to the university, which henceforth vowed to clean up its act. But I'd learn later from leading attorneys in this field, this was not a place where you wanted to be accused of misconduct.

Hence, the sentiment: The dog ate my homework. My flight was canceled. I missed my train. In my mind, I grasped futilely at any possible excuse not to participate in what felt like an inherently unfair and flawed proceeding. Indeed, I was particularly despondent about the chances of a fair hearing because of a recent telephone conversation between a top university official and one of my attorneys.

The top university official first informed my attorney it was obligated to proceed with its investigation of the accusations of misconduct. But when I reviewed the university's guidelines, I discovered it was under no obligation to do anything if I simply walked away and resigned, moved to a remote village in the Mexico countryside, or vanished into the plain ether. (My plan, by the way, at that moment.)

When my attorney relayed this, the top university official said, in effect: Yes, now that you mention it, it was true the school didn't have to do anything, but it intended to move forward with its internal investigation, no matter what; otherwise, the top university official said, the school would be blasted in the media by the attack group organized by the aforementioned employee I let go.

Another high-ranking university official confided in me

the school was particularly sensitive to the criticism, also leveled by this organized attack group, that the university wasn't doing enough about allegations of misconduct. But wait. Wasn't that like giving into the ransom demands of the bad guys? If the university was fearful of backlash from the group attacking me, unless the school went forward with its internal investigation, then didn't it stand to reason the only way for the university to avoid backlash was to find me guilty? So the verdict was already determined. Right? (That was a rhetorical question.)

I scurried to scan the fine print in university material to determine the possible punishments for alleged misconduct, which turned out to be just about anything, including suspension, demotion, stripping of tenure, and firing. Nothing in there about flogging or burning at the stake.

So it could've been worse.

After consulting with my lawyers, I decided to decline to submit to what seemed to be a rigged university investigation. But a top university official tried to coax me to the interrogation room, telling my attorney I was only accused of using inappropriate words, such as commenting on people's appearance, or asking personal questions. No one accused me of, for instance, exchanging sex for grades, the top university official said. My first thought: My goodness. Who would even think of that?

One of my attorneys said the interrogation didn't sound so bad. So I shaved. I figured I didn't have a choice, anyway.

My employer was requiring me to submit to its interrogation, and it warned me it would reach a conclusion even if I didn't participate in its investigation. Mexico wouldn't save me.

My daughter must've detected my reluctance that morning. Suddenly, she didn't feel well enough to go to school. Stomachache. Ah, the old unobservable, unmeasurable illness. And no babysitter. Too short notice. That meant my daughter would have to come with me to the interrogation.

At first, I worried it would be held against me. Too chicken to show up alone. Had to bring his ten-year-old daughter. Playing the sympathy card. (She was super cute, empirically speaking.) But then, I felt emboldened. Okay. Maybe not emboldened. But not terrified. At least not completely. I wasn't alone. My daughter would be by my side. Well, she'd be outside the closed room where I would take a verbal beating. She'd be watching *Friends* on her laptop for hours. Good enough for me. I'm not sure I could've made it without her.

A major focus of the interrogation: a chair. Some former students apparently called it a beanbag chair. It wasn't. They said I forced them to sit in that chair. I didn't. Not sure how I'd do that, anyway. There were other chairs in my office. The choice of chairs was an exercise in free will. Not a major exercise. A little one. They told the university investigator the chair in my office made them uncomfortable because of the "power differential." *What?*

There was a sameness to the language being used by the accusers. I found out later the former employee spent a good bit of time secretly soliciting my former students of years past, seeking to enlist them in the takedown. I found out later that she was represented by a major law firm, and the accusers were communicating with each other, comparing stories. I also found out "power differential" is a fancy way of saying the chair in question in my office was lower to the ground than my chair.

Picture me looking utterly bamboozled. I tried to explain to the university investigator that the chair—a futon chair, for the record—was for my kids. They came by my office quite frequently. Liked to hang out. Draw pictures with magic markers. My children were, for lack of a better term, small people. Thus, a small chair. This reasoning fell on deaf ears. The university investigator pressed: Do you continue to maintain you didn't make them sit in that chair?

I chucked the chair. In a garbage bin. Heaved it in unceremoniously. As soon as I heard about these chair allegations from the university investigator.

Most of the allegations, by the way, were at least five years old. Many were nearly a decade old. I had trouble remembering what I did yesterday. But a chair?

Then there was this Kafkaesque line of questioning from the university investigator: Are you willing to admit there was a girl in college you liked named Emily? (Now, we were talking decades ago.) Yes. Did you date her? No. Tell me the Hershey Kiss story. Okay. When I was a freshman in college, I liked a girl named Emily. We were friends. One time, we were in her dorm room. I had a Hershey's chocolate kiss in my pocket. She didn't know it. I asked her if she wanted a kiss. She said yes. I was too afraid. So I tossed her the Hershey's Kiss.

The university investigator was tapping notes into her laptop like mad. This apparently was quite an admission. A former graduate student, from nearly a decade ago, was now making the claim the Hershey's Kiss anecdote was an inappropriate story of a sexual nature. It was actually quite the opposite, a story of a nonsexual nature. Nothing happened. Not a single thing. Nada. I told this anecdote over the years as a cautionary tale. It was an example of how not to be afraid to pursue what you want in life. I checked with one of my lawyers. Recounted the anecdote. How bad was it? He scoffed. As if I bothered him with a trifling. The former graduate student, au contraire, saw the Hershey's Kiss story as an example of sexual misconduct. She also saw it as an opportunity to tell this story on TV news nearly ten years later to make the case that I was a monster. So that's what I get. I not only don't get the girl, I get publicly shamed decades later on television news for it.

I had no idea such an anecdote would cause consternation. Indeed, when I first joined the university a decade earlier, I became acquainted with a longstanding practice that suggested otherwise: at week's end, professors and graduate students in their first term at the school would stroll together over to Nevins, a local bar, to share in alcoholic beverages and regale each other with personal tales of woe. Actually, I heard other professors did more than commiserate with some students. One Northwestern professor, J. Michael Bailey, famously had two people perform a sexual act before a gallery of students agape after class. This apparently was a form of teaching. As of this writing, he still teaches there.

I was, incidentally, never told what to say—or not say—when I became a professor after leaving the *Washington Post*. How I taught and what I said, in or out of the classroom, was left entirely up to me. Nobody asked otherwise. Nobody ever came by my class to check what I was saying or doing. The total amount of guidance: Zero.

So when students began showing up unprompted at my office, I considered it an honor they wanted to know about me and trusted me enough to tell me about themselves. That included a student who told me she had suicidal thoughts. Concerned, I encouraged her to get help. She was. She also repeatedly emailed me, asking to meet with me. I obliged, meeting her on occasion, hoping it was helpful. She also asked for help with job references and job prospects after she graduated. I was happy to oblige. Now, about five years after graduating, she suddenly joined the accusers, filing a harassment complaint with the university, alleging I "pressured" her into meeting with me all those years ago. I was stunned. There was no other way to put it.

Just days before the first public attack in the news media, I heard from another former student. She emailed me to thank me profusely for the lessons learned in my class investigating wrongful convictions and working for me as an intern at The Medill Justice Project. She explained how much the experience had helped her since joining the workforce. Now that she had graduated, she was emailing me to see if there were opportunities to partner with me on any projects. She sent me a Christmas card with her posed photo on it.

But then came the attacks in the media. This former student, suddenly whipped up by the allegations, decided I was a "predator." She filed a harassment complaint against me with the university. Her unnamed accusations ran amuck in the media. Didn't matter that her allegations were anonymous. I was called a "predator" in news reports. This former student also posted on social media how she reframed her experience with me in light of the media attacks. Later, I learned she stopped responding to the university investigator's questions, thus withdrawing herself from the process. Didn't matter. There was no withdrawing "predator" from the internet.

Things get muddled in the media. People don't pay close attention. All that's left is a confusion of inflammatory words that stick.

In light of the media attacks, other former students were stirred to file complaints. The pile-on effect. Two were angry about grades they received about seven years earlier. One received a B. She thought she deserved a B+. I agreed then and gave it to her. The other received a B+. She thought she deserved an A-. I agreed then and gave it to her. Evidently, seven years later, those improved grades weren't enough. The university investigator grilled me for hours about this. I was stunned. There was no other way to put it.

Another former student, swept up in the fervor of the moment, came forward nearly a decade after being in my class to file a complaint, alleging I berated her when she received a 71 on her midterm grade that accounted for about 10 percent of her final grade. I found emails directly refuting the allegation.

A former graduate student, who had trouble understanding English, accused me of mocking her on a reporting trip to Florida. I checked my records. I wasn't in Florida. I informed the university investigator. The investigator subsequently revised the account, now telling me the alleged mockery didn't occur in Florida. The lie moved to another state. I checked my records. This former student emailed me at the end of the term, expressing the opposite sentiment, thanking me for my kindness. Didn't matter. Another former student accused me of giving her a bad job reference, though I gave her a strong recommendation, and she got the job. Didn't matter.

In the media, the number of accusers, twenty-nine in all—most anonymous—was inflated. I was notified of twenty-two who privately complained to the university about me, with at least one dropping out later. Of the twenty-one, most of their complaints centered on accusations that I was tough, or somehow mistreated them as their professor. This was a tiny fraction out of well over a thousand students with whom I interacted over a decade. And these complaints were in direct contradiction to all ten years of anonymous student evaluations at Northwestern that overwhelmingly said I was deeply caring of my students.

Indeed, I had never been accused of any mistreatment by any students at any university—not just Northwestern but at Georgetown and American universities—in any of the fifteen years I taught. Didn't matter.

In the media, I was accused of sexual assault, even though no one accused me of that. Didn't matter. No one accused me of propositioning anyone. No one accused me of exposing myself. There was nothing even remotely of the kind. The worst of the harassment accusations—of any alleged touching—came from three former students from several years earlier who had never complained before about me. But now one said I touched the tag in the back of her shirt to see what size it was to know which Medill Justice Project T-shirt to give her. The second said my hand accidentally brushed hers and I patted her on the shoulder, telling her in a paternalistic way it was going to be okay, whatever it was. The third and final said I touched her hand to see what she wrote on it with a pen, that we stood back to back to compare heights, and I hugged her.

One of those three said I sat too close to her in my office and she didn't like the way I looked at her. And yet all three of these former students sought to work with me *after* the period they were now accusing me of misconduct.

Each of these three former students also had an ax to grind. I caught one of these students using a story I edited for another class, and I did not renew her paid internship. I discovered the second student was paid for months as an intern for work that wasn't done; she too was not brought back for another internship. The third was upset after losing a paid fellowship to work with me because her status as an international student made her ineligible.

Even though I could see what was happening, I was so shocked by the allegations I felt virtually frozen in sadness. Julie-Ann, despite the crumbled state of our marriage, was more animated. Furious. She took matters in her own hands, drafting an email for me to my lawyers to distill what was happening to its essence: "An email was created by one of the accusers inviting people to contact them through an email specifically created for the purpose of generating complaints against me. This was the equivalent of putting a billboard on a highway. How many professors, staffers and others could withstand that type of scrutiny? And at the end of the day, what was the worst of the worst that they came away with? A hug, a pat and a brush of the hand."

None of this was reported in the media. It didn't matter

the allegations were false. I wasn't given a chance to defend myself. I wasn't found guilty of anything. I wanted to speak out to tell my story. But my lawyers advised me to keep my mouth shut. The university, after all, was investigating me and determining my fate. I was, they cautioned, obligated to honor the confidentiality of the process; the last thing I should do was draw the university's ire.

Most men accused of misconduct fell immediately. Many were instantly fired. Or resigned immediately. I'd been twisting in the wind for several months—I wasn't sanctioned in any way, I wasn't fired, and I hadn't resigned—while I continued to be stoned publicly online. But if I knew anything about the media from being in it for decades, there was no way to predict or control the message, especially if you were being depicted in the news as the unindicted bad guy.

I didn't know it then, but I was dead from the moment I took over The Medill Justice Project about seven years earlier. That's when it was a little organization known as the Medill Innocence Project.

Back then, several top university officials implored me to stick with the project, fighting to free the innocent, to save the organization from imminent collapse, for the sake of students and faculty, in the name of the university.

The professor who used to run the project was forced out in an ethics scandal and denounced me for not being qualified to take his place. Out of a sense of obligation to the university, to do the right thing, I took over the project, investigating wrongful convictions.

Soon after, a local tabloid ran a cover story, accusing me of not caring about helping the innocent even though that's what I did virtually every day of my life. The reporter of that story spoke to me by phone for perhaps a total of five minutes, without a hint of revealing his story angle.

About a year later, an unnamed attacker tried to get a major media outlet to write another story to take me down, accusing me of inflating my bio by saying I had been nominated for the Pulitzer Prize. I had in fact contributed to a Pulitzer-winning series but never mentioned it in my bio because I didn't want to take away from the reporter who deserved the spotlight. The university hired an attorney to defend me. That attack story never ran.

The next attack, in 2015, came from a former administrative assistant. An employee for six months, she was on what was called a corrective-action plan, probation for poor work performance. It was the last step before being fired. This assistant abruptly quit before that happened and then accused me of sexual harassment. The university investigated the matter and caught this former assistant in a number of documented lies, ruling against her. She appealed the decision to a higher authority at the university, which reviewed the matter again and found against her.

In an attempt to protect my reputation, the university went so far as to reach out to everyone who was interviewed as part of that investigation to inform them that I did nothing wrong and the matter was confidential.

The former assistant then complained to another authority. University lawyers advised me they thought it would be best to try to resolve the matter, so it wouldn't continue to be a drain on time and resources. So the university offered the former assistant what it considered a nominal amount—about $5,000 after taxes—to end the matter, sign a confidential agreement, and specifically stipulate I did nothing wrong. Further, she was forbidden from ever applying for a job at the university again. The assistant agreed.

About a year later, in 2016, an editor of an online news outlet contacted me, seeking to check a reference of a former student of mine who was seeking an internship. When I spoke with this editor by phone, I gave my former student a glowing recommendation. Pressed on her writing, I spoke well of my former student, also making the point that, for all young writers, it's a process to learn the craft of writing as a journalist. I said something along the lines of, perhaps you would understand, you sound young. The editor took immediate umbrage, accusing me of suggesting that because she was a woman, she wasn't a good writer. But I never read her writing. I didn't know if she was a good writer. In fact, I never mentioned gender in the entire conversation.

The editor tweeted about the exchange, accusing me of making sexist remarks. She didn't mention me by my name but told her tens of thousands of followers she was referring to a Northwestern professor. That prompted a round of speculation aimed at other professors, who suddenly found themselves the object of online scorn. So I sought to defuse the situation by voluntarily coming forward and identifying myself as the professor who spoke with this editor, chalking it up to a misunderstanding. My former student got the internship. I got castigated in a Twitter storm.

Soon after, the former employee I let go years earlier tried to attack me through the same local reporter who had written the cover story alleging I didn't care about helping the innocent. The former employee accused me of being mean to students. She also tried to peddle what she knew to be false: the assistant's false allegations of sexual harassment. The former employee knew the allegations were false because she was one of the people contacted by the university to specifically inform her that I did nothing wrong. The university hired another attorney to defend me. That attack story never ran.

Sometime after this, I called a top university official. Why, I wanted to know, was I subject to repeated attacks? I was merely a professor. She suggested it was partly because of the circumstances when I took over The Medill Justice Project from a popular professor, engendering a slew of enemies. I learned later the ousted professor went on to collaborate with the former employee I let go. I also learned later the former employee began communicating with the former assistant who made false allegations against me.

When I took over The Medill Justice Project, I inherited the private investigator who worked for years as a class aide with the ousted professor. That is, until the private investigator stepped down after I disapproved of some of his approaches. I learned later the private investigator encouraged some of my students to complain about me to school officials.

When the next attack came, it came again from the former employee I let go years earlier. She went with a group of others to the university to accuse me of sexual harassment and bullying. I was asked to meet with the university investigator. She told me none of the accusations, "even if true," rose to the level of a "policy violation." Thus, the university investigator said, the matter was closed. She described putting the file away in her desk drawer. She said I would never see or hear from her again.

The next day, in early February of 2018, the former employee disseminated the open letter, the attack in the media. I got a call from a top university official. The university needed to issue a public statement. A bunch of other top officials were involved in writing it. I was asked to help edit the draft. But then, suddenly, I was dropped off the email thread. I didn't know what was happening. Until some minutes later, the university issued a public statement to the media, announcing it was investigating me. That wasn't part of the draft I saw. It was added in the moments after I was dropped from the email thread.

I promptly heard from the university investigator who had told me I'd never hear from her again because none of the allegations of sexual harassment rose to the level of a policy violation. Reversing herself, she was investigating me. I'd be hearing from her again.

One of my lawyers sent a letter to the university, saying the investigator undermined her credibility, after informing me none of the allegations rose to the level of a policy violation. My attorney requested she be replaced by an impartial investigator. She wasn't. All my attorney's letter did, I feared, was anger her.

Later, through people who supported me, I obtained a copy of an email from the former employee I let go. She had secretly emailed her group of accusers on the eve of issuing their open letter attacking me in the media. In her email, she tried to address their concerns that they were not accusing me of sexual harassment; rather, some were unhappy with their experience with me as their professor. She assured them she'd rephrase the open letter to the media. But she had already provided an "embargoed" copy of the open letter to the school newspaper, even before the university determined none of the accusations rose to the level of a policy violation. She was giving the school newspaper time to prepare this takedown piece.

For what it's worth, the former employee was an excellent graduate student in one of my classes about a decade earlier. She and I got along well after she earned her degree.

But when she came to work for me at The Medill Justice Project, she sometimes bristled when I asked her to do something. She sometimes disregarded what I asked her to do. But I was to blame, too. I'd been a lone wolf for most of my career as an investigative journalist. I expected her to do what she was supposed to do because I did what I was supposed to do. I wasn't patient enough. I should have been more forgiving. I should have been more encouraging. I shouldn't have withdrawn so much. I should have engaged more. She was, after all, smart and talented in her own right. I was, in brief, a lousy boss. It took me a while to figure out how to be better.

Eventually, I did figure it out, and I got along well with my staffers for years. But not her. About a year and a half into her job, I informed her I wasn't renewing her employment appointment. All she could get then was a job in public relations, which she detested. She was being removed from the meaningful journalism she wanted to pursue. We weren't a good fit to work together, but I should have apologized, even years later, for not being more compassionate. I should have better understood what she went through, the loss. It also seemed she felt she hadn't been given enough credit for her work, so she took a good deal of credit herself for an investigation I oversaw with my students that led to an inmate being set free from prison in the wake of our findings. She did deserve credit for finding the case. I should have done more to give her that credit.

It didn't matter the former employee never accused me of misconduct before. Not when she was a graduate student nearly a decade earlier. Not years later, when I informed her that I wasn't renewing her employment. Not years after that, when she was interviewed by the university as part of the investigation of the assistant's false allegations of misconduct. But now, taking advantage of the roiling times, the former employee was suddenly accusing me of sexual harassment.

The open letter to the media highlighted the former assistant's false accusations of sexual harassment—the most inflammatory allegations, the kind that would engender widespread outrage. Indeed, those were the chief bullet points in the open letter even though the former employee knew those allegations to be false since the university had informed her that I did nothing wrong.

In the days that followed, much would be made in the media that the former assistant was paid what was erroneously reported to be about $7,500, as if it was hush money, when it was nothing of the sort. The university agreement specifically stipulated I did nothing wrong and she could never work for the university again.

For the attack to be more effective, though, it needed a group of accusers; that is, their complaints, taken individually, wouldn't have enough impact. One of the accusers said as much later in an interview with a news outlet. She was a former graduate student who said I was mean to her nearly a decade ago. I found an email from her, expressing the opposite, praising her experience in my class. Didn't matter.

It occurred to me that when you teach and interact with well over a thousand students over a decade, some won't like you. But being a professor isn't a popularity contest. Or shouldn't be, in my opinion. My feeling was—and is—you hold students accountable, you inspire them to do their best work.

The class I taught presented a particular challenge: What students did wasn't a matter of theory. What they did wasn't contained within the ivy walls of the classroom. What they— what we—did was investigate real murder cases, potentially wrongful convictions, and published our findings for the world to scrutinize.

A lot was at stake. Prisoners on death row. Inmates sentenced to life sentences. What's more, our investigations inherently challenged significant and powerful institutions: Police, prosecutors, judges, and others. And many didn't care the stories were the product of college and graduate students under the tutelage of a professor. Sometimes, powerful forces would attack our findings—or us—to try to undermine the facts we uncovered.

Before I took over The Medill Justice Project, the professor who ran it, his private investigator who worked as his aide, and their students were publicly accused of ethical misconduct. One student pretended to be a federal census worker trying to get someone's personal information.

Another posed as a ComEd utility worker. Other students were accused of flirting with sources to gain favor. Still others were accused of paying sources for information. Prosecutors demanded access to student records. Students were subjected to salacious headlines in the news.

When I took over The Medill Justice Project, my hope was to teach students to adhere to the highest ethical standards of journalism. It was, I believed, the only way.

But now, I began to question myself. Maybe I pushed students too hard. Maybe I expected too much of college and graduate students; investigative journalism, after all, was generally reserved for senior reporters who had proven themselves in the profession.

All I knew when the media barrage came was what it felt like to be wrongfully accused after spending years investigating cases of wrongful convictions.

chapter five

I'm on the ground. I can't get up. It feels like gravitational forces are grinding me into pulp, into a state of permanent inertia.

I can't move. I barely eat. I don't want to live. I think of ways of actively dying. I don't particularly like pain, however. A minor problem. It rules out jumping off a building. Too painful at the end. I could close my eyes while driving full throttle on the highway until I careen off a curve into nothingness. I try it for a blink of an eye.

Then stop.

Knowing my luck, I'd live. Or worse, hurt someone else. Not an option. My father already took the pills and the plastic garbage bag tied over the head. That idea is already gone. Scene stealer. I can't be a copycat, especially of my father. Bad enough I followed him into the same profession as a journalist and later an author. Can't just keep going with the imitation act, tying a plastic bag over my addled head. Not cool.

Offhand, on the phone, he mentions it could be worse. Oh, yeah? Yeah, you could have terminal cancer. I'd prefer to have terminal cancer. No hesitation. It isn't even a close call. It's a landslide election. Terminal cancer wins. A death not of one's own doing. Can't be blamed. Nothing to be done about it. And there's no disgrace, no permanent stain. To end the anguish, which won't relent. It's always there.

And yet, I realize others are suffering far more than me. There is so much suffering out there—from famine, war, illness, death, disease, poverty—who am I to complain? So I should just shut my trap and take my agony agreeably. Except I can't. Which makes it worse. Because I feel bad, I'm unable to manage the suffering, which makes the suffering that much worse. The wimp. It's just my measly life. An insignificant gnat on the backside of a dog of a life. It will be over before long, and even the memory of me won't last beyond a generation, maybe two. I mean, who was my great-grandfather? No idea.

Random distant memories flash before me: of Mom,

youthful, spry, bringing a candle-lit birthday cake to my highchair while I clap in delight. Of the time, as a tyke, I carefully step into a pool until my head sinks, about to be drowned, baptized in death, until saved by someone unknown. Of those mornings in high school when I insist that I'm just thinking with my eyes closed while I continue to sleep into lateness. Of 9–11, when I miss crashing into the Pentagon by one scheduled flight on the same path.

Saved for this. What was the point?

On the rare occasions I must leave the house, I look around me, observing carefree people in slow motion. I notice the lightness of step, how they laugh and chat and bubble about without the weight of permanent disgrace, how they can move about the world, through society, unburdened. I feel like crying at random moments. Tears well up when I least expect them. I see a store clerk and think how much better he has it. I think about the meaning of suffering, when it reaches the boiling point, there's sometimes an inexplicable byproduct, that of the creation of beauty in the midst of hardness, of the blues.

I wonder whether I'm losing my grasp. It isn't just my destroyed reputation. That my career is over. That my father tried to commit suicide in the middle of all of this. That we're hemorrhaging money to lawyers, and we'll probably lose the house. That my marriage is over. That I'm Quasimodo in the village. Or that I'm not even qualified to drive an Uber. It's that I can't fathom the future. Decades more of this. Of being me. I see no way out. I can't solve this math problem. I just want to *not* exist any longer.

This is what rock bottom looks like from ground level, from nose level, as it's planted in the dining room rug. But then I think of my beloved children. And dear Rosie. Nobody understands her poop schedule like I do.

Up the meds.

Okay, I'll admit, when one of my lawyer friends called around this time, I was a tad foggy, something on the order of moderately delusional. Had I been asked how much two plus two equaled at that moment, I might have come up with five. Because sometimes it does. Right?

But my attorney friend, not seeing the existential humor in my mood, asked—in mid-sentence—to speak with Julie-Ann alone. I handed the phone to her and reclined to the dining room rug while they spoke in private off to the side. She was animated. I sensed some gesticulating was involved. I could tell there was a cabal being formed. Let it. Shortly thereafter, I was looped back into the conversation. They had news for me: I wasn't functioning properly.

My attorney friend asked Julie-Ann to corroborate this. She did. Actually, it went further than that. They, the two of them, didn't have confidence I was able to function at all. She betrayed me, that stinker, by informing my attorney friend I spent my days with my face planted in the fibers of the dining room rug. Like it was his business, goodness gracious. Who doesn't have their face planted in dining room rugs? They didn't have confidence I could handle my own affairs at this juncture.

That was the word hanging in the air. Juncture. As opposed to previous junctures or future junctures when I was as capable as a caffeinated railroad engineer. Just not now.

"Oh." That was the totality of my reaction, which only reinforced their belief system about this juncture. As a result, my attorney friend strongly urged that I defer to Julie-Ann to write a note to the university investigator about my— let's call it—condition, asking for more time to prepare my defense and respond. Okay. Fine. So, she emailed, "Alec has become essentially functionless and is unable to carry out the most basic daily activities . . . To repeat, I am very concerned about Alec's personal safety."

Nice, that last bit. Especially since she frequently felt a different sentiment, wanting to verbally jab me—rightfully so, I might add—for all the hurt over the many years of our marriage. But the rest was slightly insulting. Especially the part about being essentially functionless. No pulling punches there. Couldn't have eased into it? Couldn't have offered a gentler version? That I was, perhaps, struggling. That I was, say, managing bravely to get by. Nah. Functionless. Pow. Right into the solar plexus. I should have taken umbrage. I could have protested the point about not being able to carry out the most basic daily activities. *Mon Dieu!* I mean, I wasn't in diapers. I wasn't gnawing on the furniture yet.

It's true, I stopped doing just about everything, except reading important things, such as ESPN news updates on my iPhone about the New York Yankees and tennis star Roger Federer. But, I did manage to do the laundry for a family of four. And quite essentially functionally, I might note for the record. I even folded. Thank you, Grandpa. (He once owned a clothing shop and taught me how to neatly fold a sweater, rest his soul.)

In fact, if the whole Uber driving thing didn't work out, I was beginning to come to the realization I had a shot at a career as a professional maid. Who said anything about functionless?

The university promptly called the police, which showed up at my doorstep. Tousle-haired, I opened the door, frightened children under my elbow. Yes? Just checking to make sure you're okay, sir. I'm okay. My lawyers didn't think it was okay. They called it dirty pool. They called it a university tactic, a way to cover their derriere.

I shrugged. What was I going to do? I just lived in this world; others were in charge.

Around this juncture, at the corner of rock bottom and functionless, I received a call out of the blue from an old friend, Kevin Armstrong. We hadn't spoken in months. Maybe a year or so. Hey, how are you? He spoke decibels too high for a person on the other end of the line where a face was planted in a rug. Kevin was naturally high on life. Ebullient. You could tell him his cherished Oklahoma

Sooners lost in overtime for the national championship, and I reckon he'd still have a bounce in his step.

He heard the bad news about me all the way to his home in Tulsa. He told me about a pastor who was facing similar tribulations. He wanted to know if I was okay. I'm okay. Anything I can do? No, thanks. I'd known Kevin for decades. He was one of my first editors when I was a cub reporter in southeastern Virginia where they called me a Yankee. One of the best editors I'd ever had. Patient. Smart. A kind person. And then I was led away by work to other places. I was never good about staying in touch, aloof bum that I was.

Several years after leaving Virginia, I was giving a keynote address in a cavernous auditorium in Chicago, talking about my work investigating wrongful convictions, when I heard a voice ring out during the question-and-answer session. I couldn't see who it was in the darkness. But then I recognized the booming voice. Ebullient. Kevin. He ended up inviting me to be the keynote speaker at a journalism awards ceremony he was overseeing in Tulsa in 2013. I went. We talked. He always had a passion for journalism, and Oklahoma had a criminal justice problem, boasting one of the highest incarceration rates in the nation.

So I told him he ought to do what I was doing, investigating wrongful convictions and writing about them. I was doing it from Chicago. He could do it from Oklahoma. There was no sense in trying to corner the market. There was plenty of room—and need—to help people who were out of options, who were suffering grave injustices. All it took was a desire to help—and maybe a website. Business cards, optional. I'd been proselytizing all over the country, helping students, professors, and others establish their own justice projects. And, lo and behold, Kevin went ahead. He created a nonprofit, Oklahoma Journalists for Justice, otherwise known as OKJ2. Along the way, he told me about the case of a man in Tulsa who was sentenced to life in prison for little more than a spate of purse snatchings over thirty years earlier. We ended up collaborating on that investigation, and while in Tulsa, we got to talking again. This was back in 2016, and we were sitting in his old Toyota. Not sure where we were going. I skipped the small talk—never one of my strong suits.

Instead, I mentioned something about how it was hard to understand why bad things happened to good people. I was talking about terrible crimes I came across over the years as I investigated wrongful convictions. The deep suffering of those paying for crimes they didn't commit. The inhumanity, the savage violence: I'd laid eyes on crime scene photos so horrific, so unimaginable, I just couldn't fathom how God—*if* God existed—could allow such terrible things to happen to good people.

Kevin listened without judgment and then, before I left Tulsa, handed me a book.

I glanced at the cover: *The Case for Christ*. Oh, boy. I

had no intentions of reading it. I didn't believe. I thought Jesus was a myth. In fact, I didn't believe in anything. That was one of my greatest phobias: The void. That in death, there was absolutely nothing. No memory. No afterlife in the clouds. Complete nihilism. Zippo. You die, you don't get to pass Go and collect $200. Indeed, the idea of gaping nothingness caused me to shudder in dread whenever I allowed myself to ponder the full extent of the idea.

But I have a habit. As an author, I'll read the opening of other authors' books. Just to see how they lift the curtain on their story, how they manage to ply the trade. Because if they can't find the right words, right away, to bring you into their tale, into their world—the honeymoon period, for goodness sakes—then what can you expect from the rest of the story? They won't be picking you up at the airport anymore, honey. It's kind of like one plumber observing how another fixes the pipe under the kitchen sink. Do they use a wrench or a screwdriver? Charles Dickens? A pretty good plumber. J.D. Salinger. Not bad either. What about this guy, Lee Strobel? And then a strange thing happened.

The Case for Christ didn't begat a story about Christ. It begat a story about the author, who just happened to be a Chicago journalist investigating a wrongful conviction. That was precisely what I was: a Chicago journalist who investigated wrongful convictions. Sheer coincidence, I told myself.

But maybe I should read on.

Strobel, the author, turned out to be a decent plumber,

too. In fact, he was more than that—an inveterate skeptic like me. The origin of *The Case for Christ* was that of a journalist who was determined to persuade his wife, a newly converted follower of Jesus, that it was all a myth. But in the process of doing what he knew how to do, investigative reporting, Strobel ended up doing the opposite: persuading himself of the divine existence of Jesus.

Strobel convinced me of something more basic: that Jesus did in fact exist. Not much of a revelation, I realize. But I was a newbie. It was a beginning. Until I read the book, I didn't know there was irrefutable proof—historical documentation and independent eyewitness corroboration—that Jesus of Nazareth actually walked the earth and led a small band of faithful followers, a motley crew of outcasts and misfits, teaching them a new way, until he was wrongfully convicted, crucified on the cross, and upended the world forever.

The book, incidentally, kept talking about another book. The Bible. The Gospels, in particular. Hadn't read that book, either. But as it happened, it was available. And, by this point, I was curious. Why read a book about another book about what Jesus said? Why not read the book itself? Go directly to the source. I was, after all, an investigative journalist like Strobel. Might as well see for myself what all the fuss was about. I mean, billions of people seemed to think it was pretty important.

So I determined to read the Gospels. I was a little worried, though. For one, surely, I wasn't worthy. For another,

I figured I wasn't qualified. I mean, I knew nothing. Don't you have to go to school for years for this kind of scholarship? Who said you could just pick up the Bible and read it? The audacity! For another, what if the Gospels, originally written in some ancient language, were translated into an arcane form of English? What if I didn't get all the wherefores and thou arts? Even more, what if I did get it, but it was—dare I say—a mite boring? I mean, have you read Melville's *Moby Dick*? Let me just put it this way: It's a classic but the art of storytelling has evolved over the years. We don't just describe, say, an inanimate object for pages.

But here's the thing. The Bible isn't boring. I think I did get the Gospels. The four accounts, recorded just a matter of decades after the crucifixion, told of the remarkable existence and works of Jesus. Four accounts of the same inspiring story. From four different angles. And a singular fact stood out to me: Everything Jesus said more than two thousand years ago has stood the test of time.

Jesus didn't say anything, with the benefit of history, which turned out to be biased, or unintentionally discriminatory. Not a single faux pas. Not one mean-spirited word. Not even close. Everything Jesus said more than two thousand years ago applied precisely to yesterday, today, and tomorrow about love and forgiveness.

It wasn't like what I'd seen and heard from people who, for instance, grew up with institutionalized racial segregation in the South; they told me it was just the way it was.

They hadn't questioned it. Because they grew up with it. Were imbued in it. Couldn't see the forest in the middle of which they stood: that racism was accepted as a way of life. Let's not forget, women once were prohibited from voting—worse, they were physically harmed for fighting for that basic right less than a century ago—and yet such fundamental discrimination was practiced as the norm of society.

Jesus didn't speak ill of anyone a couple of millennia ago. Jesus treated children with kindness at a time when children were often abused. Jesus treated women with respect at a time when women were decidedly considered second-class citizens. Jesus embraced lepers, tax collectors, and fishermen alike. At a time when the prevailing credo was an eye for an eye—vengeance—Jesus preached a revolutionary idea: Love thy enemy.

I kept reading. I read the rest of the New Testament. By the end, I reached a decision: My children would grow up with Jesus in their lives. And why not? What was not to like about love and forgiveness? This was kind of a big deal for me. My worldview as a skeptical journalist was largely shaped by my father, a hard-driving journalist who didn't espouse any particular faith. He was ethnically Jewish but, with all due respect, one of the least Jewish people I knew. He went through the motions, sending me to a reform temple, which was relaxed about the rules, to have me bar mitzvahed, but I didn't understand the Hebrew words I was asked to memorize, and I rejected the religion.

Besides, we celebrated Christmas, and if you wanted verification of where we stood in the grand scheme of things, all my father's wives (and almost wives) were Christian, except my mother. She was Japanese, which might have seemed like being Jewish at times, given all the forced feedings. Eat, eat. But not to Jews. Doesn't matter if your father is Jewish. Your mother must be Jewish for you to be Jewish, according to the rules. This was once proven to me when a group of Hasidic Jews emerged from an abruptly halted van and fanned out across a city street. One quickly stopped before me and asked if I was Jewish; I began to stammer, he peered at me dubiously, and then he asked if my mother was Jewish. When I said she was Japanese, a shadow of disappointment came over him, and off he dashed, looking for an authentic prospect.

Now, of course, if it was Hitler who hopped out of the Hasidic van and asked me the same question, I'd be stuffed in a gas oven. As for my mother, she was a bit more equivocal; she was either a Buddhist or Shintoist, though I'm not sure it mattered when it came to trying to place me in a neat little box.

Years ago, when I was young, I rejected Jesus when I dated a true believer. And still later, I dismissed the possibilities of signs, including a play I wrote, staged at the National Theatre in Washington, D.C., in the early 2000s when I was an investigative reporter at the *Washington Post*. I titled the play, "The Carpenter Who Wouldn't Leave." When I told my friend Kevin about that, he raised his eyes portentously. Meanwhile, I wasn't aware I had been unintentionally echoing some of the underlying tenets of Jesus as I crisscrossed the United States, giving talks over the years about my work as an investigative journalist. I coined the term "fair check" to encourage journalists to not only check their stories for accuracy but to check their articles for fairness. I would talk about what I called "the journalism of compassion," a concept I wrote about in one of my other books. We, as journalists, needed to be sensitive to the impact of our journalism. We needed to put other people before ourselves. When sources for our stories wanted to change their minds, when they wanted to withdraw their quotes or involvement before publication, even if they promised us, we needed to honor their wishes. We needed to let go, even if it was to our own detriment. There must be limits to our own ambitions.

On more than one of my investigations at the *Washington Post*, I told my editor I was removing passages I feared would harm sources. One such passage was to lead a three-part investigation I spent months tracking down. I didn't want to delete all that hard work. But a source told me that he worried people would think he had provided that sensitive information. I pointed out to my source he didn't give me that information. While true, he noted people would think he gave it to me because so few had access to it. Good point. So I deleted it. And my editor, Larry, never hesitated in backing me. A good man. He understood. This was the lesson I tried to impart to my students as well.

Joyce got it. A graduate student of mine nearly a decade ago, I still have a frayed printout of what she read aloud on the last day of class: "Alec Klein is no ordinary professor. More than investigative reporting, he has imparted to us a code of behavior. Every class he poses ethical questions, and urges us to search our consciences for the answer. Some things I took away from my time in Professor Klein's class: Never use deceit to obtain what you need for a story, there is always another way. Never lie to your sources, or make them false promises. Make little promises. Keep them. This is how you'll win the confidences of your sources, and make a reputation for yourself as being fair and objective. Never put a story above people. Journalism can have terrible consequences, and as journalists we must recognize our power. People have lost their livelihoods, their families, the community's respect, and sometimes people have even killed themselves because of a published article. We must be careful of what we write and how we write it. Professor Klein, you have given us the tools to go out and do journalism far beyond what we have done here today. On behalf of the class, I want to thank you."

Joyce wasn't trying to curry favor for a better grade. She decidedly did her own thing. Unfiltered, Joyce once let me know a role-playing exercise in class hadn't worked almost immediately after it hadn't worked. It failed to make the point about reporting; it only illustrated I was a poor actor. Joyce was right. Even before she surprised me with her class postscript, she had a way about her that set her apart. Once, she wanted to show me one of her favorite places to eat lunch near campus, a Korean greasy spoon that doesn't exist anymore. I still remember the investigation she did for class. It was about how companies sell bottled juices at the supermarket, touting them as having less sugar and calories. But what she found was they just reduced the amount of juice, placing more water in the bottles.

In all my years of teaching, well over a decade, Joyce was the only student who ever asked me if she could stand up on the last day of class and make a prepared statement before her classmates and me. But that was Joyce. She never mentioned her faith, or whether she had any. But if there was anyone who had a lightness in her, an almost ethereal quality about her, it was Joyce. Not long after the class ended, Joyce passed away. She was in her early twenties. Perhaps she was too good for this world.

But then, maybe I was just trying to comfort myself about the meaning of her death. This was when I didn't know what to think.

I was a non-believing mutt. And, technically speaking, a heathen.

Only after reading *The Case for Christ* had I come around to believing Jesus existed. I wasn't sure about the miracles, though. Walking on water? Loaves and fishes out of thin air?

Rising from the dead? I wasn't ready for all that. But I saw a miracle in something more elemental: the message of Jesus, which was profoundly good. To love, to forgive.

Another miracle: I came around to having my children learn the life and lessons of Jesus. At bedtime, I'd regale them with stories from the Bible. How crowds clamored to meet Jesus, to listen to him preach, to hear him minister about being kind and gentle, to turn the other cheek, to be healed. How Jesus predicted Peter would deny knowing Jesus three times in the final hours. How, before it happened, Jesus forgave Peter, who would atone by spending the rest of his life spreading the Gospel until he was crucified for it. How Paul, a persecutor of Jesus's followers, became one of Jesus's greatest champions. How Paul went on to placidly predict everything would be fine in the midst of panic on a ship in a furious storm as the others abandoned all hope, tossing goods overboard. How Paul crisscrossed wide swaths of the world, energetic old soul that he was, planting the seeds of the church of Christ.

My children thirsted for these biblical tales, urging me to tell them more, more, Daddy, more, until I ran out of stories of Jesus and realized I better start reading the other book. The Old Testament. A lot of good stories in there, too.

By the way, both old and new parts of the Bible documented the evils of false allegations. Thou shalt not bear false witness is one of the Ten Commandments. Think of the intricate story of Joseph, wrongfully accused and imprisoned. Think of the central story of Jesus, who was wrongfully convicted and crucified. I'd learn all of this later.

In the meantime, my children were baptized, which meant I sat glued to the church pews alone, while they, Julie-Ann, and the rest of the congregation went up to accept the body of Christ. Occasionally, I'd slip into a church alone when no one was looking. Any denomination was fine with me. I'd get on my knees, bow my head, clasp my hands, close my eyes, and pray.

I wasn't sure anyone was listening. Wasn't sure I was worthy. But still, I would thank God. I would pray for forgiveness. I would pray to forgive. Almost unconsciously, I found myself gathering signs of the cross in my daily life: on a keychain, a padfolio, a backpack. Okay. Not exactly the cross. They were the logos of the Swiss Army Knife. But they sure looked like the cross to a novice like me.

This was, I suppose, partly Kevin's fault. He did give me that book about Jesus years earlier. And now, here he was again, in 2018. Ebullient as ever. Calling to ask me how I was in the midst of my ordeal, at the corner of rock bottom and functionless. You ought to come out here. Tulsa? Yeah, I have a friend I want you to meet. Oh? Name is Eric. Told him all about you. Hopefully not everything, ha, ha. He wants your help. With what? Eric wants to create a justice project. To help people who are wrongfully convicted. He's a good guy.

I was sure he was. I wasn't so sure, however, I could help

at this juncture. I couldn't, after all, help myself. I had been entombed for months, barely leaving the house, a practical shut-in, dusty face buried in a dusty rug, immersed in meds, while enduring a public stoning in the media as I submitted to a still-ongoing university investigation.

One of my attorneys explicitly told me not to go to Oklahoma. She said it would undermine my case and the note Julie-Ann had sent to the university investigator. That I was "essentially functionless" and needed more time to prepare my response. I might be under surveillance. Because that's how these things played out. This was hardball. If I was observed going to Oklahoma, it would prove I was a lying sack of dung. I was perfectly functional because I could get on an airplane and help people who were wrongfully convicted. This, the lawyer said, would anger the university, and, thus, I would be in even more peril, especially at this delicate stage of the process when my fate hung in the balance. Another of my lawyer friends concurred unequivocally: "Do—not—go."

So I decided to go.

Maybe to get out of Dodge. Maybe because what the heck. The lawyer friend said I was being "selfish." I feebly tried to make the point that people who are wrongfully convicted need help. He said I needed to help myself first, which, in turn, would help my family. He said it was reckless for me to go. The other lawyer, recognizing I was going, no matter what, warned me, in no uncertain terms, that I was not to tell anyone, except my family, I was going. No one was to tell anyone I was going. No social media. No emails. All radio silence. Okay. Fine. I wasn't worried.

I mean, what do you have to lose when you feel like you've already lost almost everything? Here was the real concern when I left town: Who was going to walk Rosie?

chapter six

When I step out of the house, luggage in hand, I blink in the light, as if emerging from a darkened cave after deep hibernation.

I don't feel particularly functional. Okay. I feel essentially functionless. I'm slightly disoriented. It feels like I'm stepping onto the moon, not quite sure what to expect. Whether I'm on solid ground, or whether I'll be swallowed up. I'm mute. I don't know if words will come out. There's the look, too: glassy-eyed.

I feel like waving to unseen eyes observing me from the

bushes. Then don't. Photoshoot away. They are right. I don't know what I'm doing. And just in case I'm lacking any equilibrium, shortly after I touch down in Tulsa, Julie-Ann sends me an ominous text; she will "never forgive" me if my trip jeopardizes everything with the university. No pressure. Help worthy people get out of prison but don't get caught doing it. I don't respond. I'm trying to get my bearings.

I am, after all, a stranger in a strange land, a Martian in cowboy country. There's something exotic to me about the Oklahoma countryside. Wide open space. I'm a city boy. I grew up between sentries of high rises, in the shadow of concrete, in an apartment where you placed the garbage can outside the backdoor and when I retrieved it later, the garbage was gone—presto—like a magic trick. I'm charmed by the Oklahoma twang. Y'all is a good invention. It rolls off the tongue effortlessly. I want to say it. But I haven't earned the right yet. I want a pair of cowboy boots. I'm particularly taken by Braum's, a local restaurant chain with excellent soft-serve ice cream.

I'm even more enamored with the QT. It's a convenience store to locals. But to me, it's a wonder. Especially the icy Freezoni drink. Pure sugar. You want pizza? We got pizza. You want gas? We got gas. Basically, the QT has everything, which is why I find myself wandering the aisles, looking for nothing in particular.

But the best part: I'm anonymous. Nobody knows who I am. Nobody cares. Nobody asks. Everyone's nice. I can move freely about Tulsa without bumping into someone who casts a withering look of condemnation.

That includes Eric, my friend's friend. Introduced by Kevin, Eric is a broad-shouldered Tulsan sitting behind a big old desk, slightly shielded by a framed Teddy Roosevelt quote. Here in downtown Tulsa, his cell phone's ringing off the hook, so I occupy myself by reading the iconic former president's famous quote:

> It is not the critic who counts; not the man who points out how the strong man stumbles, or where the doer of deeds could have done them better. The credit belongs to the man who is actually in the arena, whose face is marred by dust and sweat and blood; who strives valiantly; who errs, who comes short again and again, because there is no effort without error and shortcoming; but who does actually strive to do the deeds; who knows great enthusiasms, the great devotions; who spends himself in a worthy cause; who at the best knows in the end the triumph of high achievement, and who at the worst, if he fails, at least fails while daring greatly, so that his place shall never be with those cold and timid souls who neither know victory nor defeat.

I'm going to like Eric. When he gets off the phone, he doesn't ask me about my disgrace. I know he knows. He knows I know he knows. But he's a licensed private detective. So he knows his way around a conversation. We talk about other stuff. High on the list: He wants to figure out how we can immediately free inmates who have been excessively sentenced, some for decades—others for life—in a state notorious for locking 'em up and throwin' away the key. In other words, can we do the impossible?

Oklahoma happens to be the epicenter of imprisonment, owning the unenviable distinction of having the highest incarceration rate in the United States—and the world, with the possible exception of North Korea, which doesn't report its numbers because it's a nation run by a dictator with a bad haircut.

Oklahoma arrived at this dubious distinction just about the time I landed in Tulsa. Oklahoma leaped over Louisiana as number one in the prison world. Suddenly, I'm not thinking of my own problems. I have a new problem. A bigger problem. I have someone else's problem: How do we immediately help prisoners who deserve another chance at freedom?

Even more, how do we help these inmates when the options are decidedly limited? Investigating wrongful convictions can take years before the vital breakthrough, even if you uncover the revelatory evidence proving their innocence. I know this from experience; in one case, years ago, we found the key eyewitness who said authorities got the wrong guy who was nonetheless convicted of murder and sentenced to life in prison. Prosecutors were not amused by our inconvenient discovery. It took three years before the case got real consideration.

So now what?

I identified a long shot possibility: Parole. What if we could help inmates who were up for parole once a month? Who deserved parole? But might not make it without help? There was only one tiny conundrum: The Oklahoma parole board, as it turned out, was comprised of well-known hard-liners: two former prosecutors, a former police officer, and a crime victim advocate. That was four out of the five parole board members. But you couldn't obtain your freedom from this board without at least three votes. And you might only get one vote, if you're lucky. The fifth parole board member was a minister. The future was etched in the past: The voting statistics showed a simple truth, that if you were a prisoner, it was difficult, by any measure, to win your freedom in this state.

I couldn't be functionless. I had to be functional. Right away. Sitting at a big conference table, I made a phone call. I contacted the head of the Oklahoma parole board, who miraculously picked up the line when I asked a cheerful assistant to speak with the boss. This wasn't my New York, deary, where you'd be fortunate to find a phone number that led you down a byzantine path into an automated hell bereft of human life.

I began the conversation with DeLynn Fudge, the head of the parole board, with a caveat: "Brace yourself," I told her. "I'm about to ask you a dumb question." She laughed. I don't think she was expecting that confession. I then proceeded to ask her a dumb question. Actually, multiple dumb questions. I was trying to figure out how the parole system worked in Oklahoma. I wanted to understand not just the nuts and bolts but the nuances. To get a better idea about how to help inmates who needed help, who deserved a second chance. She answered all my questions with patience and clarity. I instantly liked her.

I also instantly liked my team working with me in Tulsa. Not just my old friend, my old editor, Kevin. And Eric, the private eye, who continued to not ask me about my disgrace in another state. The small team also included Rhonda Bear, who might actually have been a saint. She had been a drug addict and dealer before she found Jesus. Now, after serving time, she created thirteen transitional homes for women emerging from prison. Now, Rhonda ran a coffee shop, She Brews, employing ex-cons. I immediately liked her.

On the team, there was also Trish Davis, a volunteer who got bored winning club tennis championships, who wanted to do something meaningful in her life. She cursed like a drunken sailor and asked pointed questions like a veteran investigative reporter. I instantly liked her.

And then there was Kate Bartholomy, a local college student who worked part-time. All she did was get everything right away, no matter how poorly I articulated—she was so smart. I instantly liked her.

I immediately liked Oklahoma, too. I was practically ready to hitch my U-Haul and move here. But first I needed to come up with an effective system to help inmates immediately get out of shackles. We'd start with women because of the obvious urgency: Oklahoma had the highest incarceration rate among women in the nation for nearly thirty years. *Twice* the national average, which meant women were in big trouble here.

Furthermore, I'd identify inmates who committed nonviolent crimes. Because they represented less of a threat to society than, say, prisoners who killed and maimed people, which, incidentally, wasn't looked upon with forgiveness by the parole board.

I'd find cases involving drugs, for instance. Methamphetamines, I learned, was huge here. Called "shake and bake" because it was so easy to make. It was sometimes called "manufacturing" drugs but wasn't. Too romantic a notion, if it could be said. These cases weren't about police raids of manufacturing plants where scientists in white lab coats were caught red-handed concocting truckloads of drugs. These were cases involving people caught with small ounces of meth.

Not good, to be sure. But did they deserve twenty years in prison for it? Or thirty years? Or life? In some cases, that's what they got. So I'd identify those inmates. I'd find them by sifting through scores of pages of monthly parole dockets filled with coding attached to each inmate—a modern

hieroglyphics—that took a while to translate. But how?
I got lucky. I met an expert named Lynn Woodward
at a local meeting of C.U.R.E., Citizens United for
Rehabilitation of Errants. Most were family members of
prisoners. Lynn's ex-husband was convicted of murder and
sent away for life. While he sat languishing in prison, Lynn
devoted years sitting in parole board meetings, taking notes
in her carefully constructed three-ring binder, to better
understand how to bring mercy to her ex-husband.

In the process, Lynn, it seemed to me, knew everything
about the Oklahoma criminal justice system. I contacted
Lynn every so often. Just have a little question or two. She'd
chuckle. Because she knew a little question or two would
turn into about a hundred questions, which would turn into
an hour-long conversation.

I'd also contact the prisoners if I could. But even when
I located them, prison telephone systems were—how shall I
put it?—not terribly user-friendly. This wasn't, as they say,
the Holiday Inn. But if I got to inmates, I'd talk with them
and learn more about their cases.

I'd also independently check records. Lots of records.
To vet their cases. Here, my experience as an investigative
reporter was particularly helpful; I'd been steeped in the
criminal justice system elsewhere, so I had an understanding
of what records I could get my hands on. I'd pull DOC—
Department of Correction—records from the web. To
better grasp their criminal past. I'd tap ODCR—on demand

court records. To delve further into the weeds of what they did that got them in trouble. How, for instance, did the crime or crimes unfold? Were there mitigating circumstances? Poverty? A violent boyfriend? An addiction? Prison often warehoused. In many cases, it didn't treat so much. Drug addicts needed help, not incarceration, in my opinion.

Meanwhile, I'd request public records of the Oklahoma Pardon and Parole Board, citing Oklahoma laws, to obtain internal investigative reports. This, too, was my bailiwick as an investigative journalist. I was familiar enough with the system to know how to employ open-records requests. I wrote a fancy letter with big five-dollar words. These records would help me better understand whether inmates stayed out of trouble while in prison. Called misconducts. If you got an A or B misconduct, it wasn't good. It might have meant a prisoner mouthed off to a prison guard. But that wasn't nearly as bad as an X misconduct, which could have indicated an inmate, for instance, hurled a large metal lock into the face of another inmate.

Then I'd try to figure out their future. I'd track down their family, friends, and others, using proprietary databases. It's downright scary what you can find out about almost anyone in this day and age. You can find out, for instance, where they live, where they used to live, their neighbors, how they registered to vote—heck, whether they have a fishing license and a lot more.

In my case, I was more interested in finding people who

could speak to the character of the inmates I was trying to help. Who could tell me if there was a support system in place if the inmates were granted parole. Faith and family. If they had a job waiting for them. Or a place to live.

The only problem, as I saw it at this point, was our organization was new. We didn't have a track record. We'd just coined the name of the nonprofit, Another Chance Justice Project. We'd come up with little more than a nifty little logo, which would mean little to the Oklahoma parole board, especially if we were advocating for inmates we felt deserved a second chance at freedom.

I figured we'd need some help. We needed other organizations to add their voice to ours. Well-respected Oklahoma groups. In the end, I was able to enlist three other non-profits. And then based on my research, I drafted a letter from all of us to the parole board, urging its five members to grant parole to the first nine inmates I identified, who deserved another chance.

I had no idea if this was going to work. In fact, I was pretty darn sure it wouldn't. I told the small team at Another Chance Justice Project—Eric, Kevin, Rhonda, Trish, and Kate—we'd be lucky if the parole board granted freedom to one of the nine inmates. We might not even get a single woman out of prison. This wasn't about me. This was about other people who needed help. In other words, this was important to me. I was worried. There was only one thing to do: Wander the aisles of the QT.

chapter seven

I wake up early, sandwiched in bed between two dogs. One, Rufus, is big and young, half on top of me. The other, Boomer, is tiny and old, curled up under my left arm.

I was assured this wouldn't happen. I'd be left alone if I slept in the guestroom. That's where I am. I'm dog-sitting at the Tulsa home of my friend Kevin's younger daughter and husband. They're on vacation.

It occurs to me this situation is probably my fault. Probably has something to do with my impromptu stop the night before at PetSmart to pick up a delectable selection of high-end dog treats. "Blue Bits Natural Soft-Moist Training Treats." "Little-Jacs Small Dog Training Treats Made with Fresh Chicken Liver."

Rufus and Boomer gobbled them and completely ignored their regular dog food. I have to admit, I didn't blame them. The regular dog food didn't look particularly appetizing. Dry and workmanlike. Not tasty and tempting like the dog treats. I'd have gone for the treats, too. Almost did.

Only now, I'm living with the consequences, as Rufus and Boomer, wide awake, tails wagging like crazy, are ready to pounce on another round of the good stuff for breakfast. I'm feeling mildly guilty. Hopefully, Kevin's daughter and husband won't be annoyed that I'm spoiling Rufus and Boomer.

And what of Rosie? Is it okay I slept with two other dogs? Does it matter it came as a complete surprise to me? I had no memory of their arrival in the bed. It was perfectly innocent.

I shake off the situation. No time. I have to shower and shave. I button up a white-collared shirt, slip on dark slacks and a blue blazer. I climb into Kevin's old Toyota—a loaner for the day—and drive the two hours down to Oklahoma City to the monthly parole board meeting. I'm about to find out whether the experiment is a total failure.

A sense of doom pervades my being as I hurtle down the highway, self-doubt mounting as I pull into the parking lot, and make my way to the fenced-in entrance of the parole board. Why did I think I could do this? Where did I get the gumption to try to help these inmates? Who did I think I was, Mr. Essentially Functionless?

In the middle of my self-loathing, I bump into a passerby in the parking lot. There's something intrinsically kind about her. A modest smile. Wisdom in her eyes, which evidenced she'd seen a lot, experienced a great deal. Not sure why we stop to acknowledge each other. Doesn't happen in New York, where you keep your head down, staring blankly at the cracked asphalt. For years, I averted my gaze in the elevator in the apartment building where I lived as a kid, so I never knew my neighbors. But we're in Oklahoma, and people are polite here.

Turns out, the stranger in the parking lot is named Kathy Peacock. Also turns out, she isn't a total stranger; she's a close personal friend of Rhonda, one of my colleagues at Another Chance Justice Project. They served time together. Now they work together. What are the chances? Dare I ask myself if there is time for such minor divine intervention? I skip the usual pleasantries, immediately gushing to Kathy about my fears.

It all comes tumbling out: That I'm about to fail nine inmates who are up for parole. Nine women who deserve another chance. Kathy gives me an amiable smile. It's as if she expected this nearly complete stranger to put on a display of unvarnished neuroticism in the middle of the parole board parking lot. She asks if she can hold my hands and if I'd mind if we pray to Jesus.

I don't. I'm not exactly a touchy-feely guy, but I can use all the help I can get, so hold hands, we do, this person I just met in the parking lot. My eyes are shut tight. Kathy's praying eloquently now. I think I hear Scripture. I try to focus on the words, their meaning. About finding strength. About relying on faith. About letting go. I'm feeling my mind unclench. And then it's over: Amen.

When I enter the building, I find myself in a little foyer where I'm greeted by a friendly guard who waves a wand over my entire body to check for weapons. I'm weaponless. Then she scoots me over to a fenced-in area behind which a dog approaches, sniffing me, arms outstretched, splayed against the fence, for drugs. I'm drugless. I have a feeling, without the fenced-in area, the dog would've eaten me for breakfast. As is, I'm free to pass along.

I enter a cavernous room. Nothing fancy about it. Reminds me of a classroom, only bigger and more barren. Just an assemblage of functional chairs, some unadorned tables, and a gathering of powerful people up front: the five-member parole board.

I take a seat a few rows back. No need to call attention to myself. Even though the place is practically empty. I steal a glance around. I'd been expecting a crowd. Family and friends of inmates. A throng of supporters. Maybe even handmade signs. But no. Just me and a couple of other stragglers, neither of whom is from an inmate's family, as it turns out. Every member of the parole board takes note of my presence, eyeing me warily. I try to nod solemnly in respect to the occasion. Somehow, though, I get the feeling it's painfully obvious I'm not from Oklahoma. I'm a half-Japanese Martian.

I take a pen out, poised to take notes, which only draws more attention. Nobody else is taking notes. The meeting comes to order. There's a discussion of parole business. It goes over my head. I have no idea what they're talking about. My hands are sweaty.

But then they get down to the real business at hand: voting on the fate of scores of inmates who are up for parole. Yearning for their freedom, they aren't here to speak for themselves. Only a small number of prisoners have earned the privilege of what's called a personal appearance—via video from prison—and for two of the nine inmates I'm helping, that happens tomorrow. Most, they are names on paper, a prison number, a six-digit DOC number.

Their slim chances of freedom arrive today under what's called a "jacket review." I hear names called out. Then votes. It goes fast, names dispatched one after another. It goes so fast, I draw a diagram of the parole board members, the better to record each of their votes as it tumbles forward. Before today's ceremony, they've already considered the cases, reviewed the files, pondered how they will vote. Down the line, it goes: No. No. No. No. No. There's a lot of noes. A rare yes. Solitary. Futile.

I'm not liking this. I want more yeses. I pick up on the

rhythm of the voting unfolding even before it unfolds. I silently mouth the word "no" a millisecond before a parole board member says no. It doesn't take long before I can predict with certainty how they will vote: No. I'm batting a thousand. But then I hear a name I recognize. One of the inmates for whom I wrote a letter of support. I freeze. Hold breath.

Yes.

Just like that. And another yes. And another. The parole board just set her free. Excitedly, I look around. There's no one to acknowledge. Still a mostly empty, unadorned room. No one to high five. I want to jump out of my chair and whoop it up. I want to run over to the parole board members and shake their hands, personally thanking them. But I'd get tackled by the guards lurking behind me and sent to jail. Which would be inconvenient since I'm not supposed to be there, an essentially functionless person.

So I sit tight, stone faced. Until I hear the name of the next inmate for whom I wrote a letter of support. She flies through, free as a bird. Just like that. Five-oh. No dissent. The parole board, that notorious gathering of hardliners, is suddenly looking a bit warm and cuddly. Might I say Teddy Bear-ish? Okay. Maybe too much. But I'm liking them even more as they vote to grant the freedom of yet another inmate for whom I wrote a letter of support. And another. And another. Five women. All set free.

I'm almost relaxing when something goes awry. I'm

waiting for the board to vote on two other inmates whose cases I researched and supported for parole.

Nothing.

Their names never come up for a vote. The meeting ends. I make my way over to DeLynn, the head of the parole board. She's accustomed to my dumb questions by now. I politely ask another. "What happened to these two inmates? Why didn't they come up for a vote as scheduled?" I was sure they deserved another chance. They earned their parole. I'm ready to state my case, to unfurl all of my research about the injustices of the system, when DeLynn checks her notes and puts a kibosh on the whole speech. Both prisoners were just slapped with misconducts. One got into a fight with another inmate. The other disrespected a prison guard.

Me: Fish-mouthed.

A fight, that's serious. Parole is automatically off the table. But disrespecting a prison guard? Well, actually, she tallied two minor misconducts right before her parole hearing. It was enough to strike her from the docket. She wouldn't be considered for parole. She'd have to wait another year until the board would consider freeing her. I didn't know what to say. I had nothing to say. I thanked DeLynn and trudged off.

All I could think about, barely aware as I wandered back to the parking lot, was: *What went wrong?* I spoke with this inmate at length, multiple times by phone. We went over everything. We reviewed all the programs she completed in prison to better herself, to give herself a real shot at freedom, to give her a better chance at success on the outside, to overcome her addiction, her circumstances.

She'd already lost so much. Her child. Who never knew her. She gave up her child for adoption when she was just a young, desperate mother with few options. She wept when we talked about her child. We went over the earnest letter she wrote to the parole board, talking about how much she regretted her actions, how much she'd changed.

I spoke with her mother, who wrote a letter by hand to the parole board, explaining her own addiction and time in prison, and how she was clean herself, and ready to help her daughter upon her release. She had a place to live, a job waiting for her. It was all there, including other letters of support I enlisted from family, friends, and community leaders. And now. This.

Only later did I learn the truth. At the last minute, she sabotaged her parole. She had a girlfriend in prison and didn't want to leave her.

Trish, my colleague at Another Chance Justice Project, called. "How'd it go?" "Okay." I recited the facts. Five of the seven inmates we helped earned their freedom. The other two we helped would come up the next day for personal appearances via video at the parole board.

"Wait. What? Five? Free?" Trish practically screamed in delight into the phone, tossing out some well-appointed curse words for good measure. "How do you feel?"

"Humbled," I said. "Thankful." (And relieved.) "What's wrong with you? This is great!" It's true, the experiment worked. We did what we set out to do as a fledgling non-profit, which was to help inmates gain their freedom immediately. I felt terrible.

Subdued, I explained I needed to call the mother of the inmate who torpedoed her own parole. I didn't know why then. I just knew it happened. Or didn't happen. She wasn't free, even though she should be. Trish sounded mildly annoyed on the other end of the line. She wanted more enthusiasm for the Big Moment. She was right. I apologized. I was never good at enjoying successes. I could always remember the failures.

I told her I'd call her later. I had to call the mother. She couldn't make it to the parole board meeting. Too far from her home. She had no way of getting there. But I knew the mother of this inmate was waiting anxiously to find out whether her daughter was free. I knew she would be devastated. I knew I didn't want to make this call. So I called.

Hi. It's Alec. I just wanted to let you know what happened at the parole board meeting. What happened? She didn't make it. I'm sorry. Oh. Silence ensued. I explained her daughter was stricken from the docket because of misconducts. Her mother's voice got real quiet: I understand. I tried to think of something positive to say. She'll come up for parole next year. We can help her then. Her voice got even smaller: Okay. Mine too: I'm sorry. Thank you.

There wasn't anything else to say, except I felt completely useless.

But that was self-evident. Essentially functionless. So I let it go.

I worried, though, about this inmate's mother. She went through personal hell herself and came out of it on the other side, had been clean for years, drug-free. And I just hoped what happened to her daughter, how her parole imploded, wouldn't set her back. There wasn't anything I could do. I tried to console myself that evening with a jaunt over to the QT, where I aimlessly trolled the aisles until ordering an extra-large pepperoni pizza.

When I got back to the place where I was dog-sitting, Boomer and Rufus looked like they urgently needed a bite. I consoled them with high-end treats. Nobody seemed particularly pleased.

That's when the phone rang. Two lawyers. It was late in the evening. They were giving me an update, which was that things were not good back in Illinois. Still. They also wanted to know how it was going in Oklahoma. I told them. Five women were set free. There were general words of congratulations: yada yada. Now the real deal: They reminded me to keep my mouth shut about my whereabouts. Not a problem. I wasn't feeling verbose.

The next day, the final two inmates for whom I wrote letters of support were set free. It didn't occur to me to appreciate the moment. I was tasked with a way to help free excessively sentenced inmates. It didn't occur to me that, in the midst of my suffering, I was drawn to a place of far greater suffering, the epicenter of mass incarceration in the world.

Only later, when I peered up at the big sky in Oklahoma, did I come to truly appreciate the place, the way sunshine illuminated a dappling of clouds, like a painting, oil on wide open canvas. Only then did I think of Oklahoma in a different way. More like God's country.

Whatever it was, I told Eric, the head of the fledgling nonprofit, where to go to greet prisoners walking to their freedom. I asked not to be mentioned in any way when he spoke with the media or anyone else. I asked him to leave me off the nonprofit's website, at least for the time being. I promised him if my presence caused any problems—any blowback—on the nonprofit, I'd immediately step aside.

All this time, I hadn't given any particular thought to my official role. I thought I was brought to Tulsa to help. Kind of like a temporary consultant. A temporary stealth consultant. A temporary stealth consultant who was disgraced and couldn't be mentioned in public. My colleagues at Another Chance Justice Project saw it otherwise. The nonprofit was formed to help give people another chance. As it turned out, my old and new friends were giving me another chance, too.

As I prepared to leave Tulsa, I had a long talk with Boomer and Rufus. I explained I was leaving behind a virtual cornucopia of high-end treats. They sat there, looking up at me quizzically. Boomer looked especially bothered. Maybe it was just my imagination. He did have that scruffy old hangdog look. I'd miss it.

chapter eight

I'm standing at the gate. It's baking hot, especially inside my blue blazer. I'm handing over my ID badge to a prison guard. She's inspecting it. I'm informing her it's a bad photo of me. She's not smiling. But she's letting me through the iron gate, into Dr. Eddie Warrior Correctional Center, about an hour outside Tulsa.

I'm back in town, along with Eric, the head of our fledgling nonprofit, Another Chance Justice Project. We've gone through a daylong training session through the Oklahoma Department of Corrections, which makes us, according to

our badges, DOC volunteers. The upshot of the training:
The answer to almost every question is no. Especially if the
question is coming from an inmate.

We're here as representatives of a program called
"Women in Transition." It's part of a faith-based initiative.
It's intended to help women inside prison gain life skills and
then mentor them once they're outside prison. The program
is run by Rhonda, my friend and nonprofit colleague who,
I increasingly suspect, is actually an angel, so devoted is she
to help others in need, so devoted is she to Christ. Rhonda
has already warned me what to expect, how to act and, in
particular, what *not* to do.

A former prisoner, Rhonda can size you up in an Okie
second. She's already got me figured out. I'm a sucker. She
doesn't say this. Because she's too nice. But I can see it written
all over her appraising face. She's told me the cautionary tale
of a man of faith who fell in love with a prisoner and got
into a lot of trouble. A—lot—of—trouble. In fact, Rhonda
told me this tragic story three times. She's told me not to fall
for hard-luck stories, warning me, that for all the wonderful
women behind bars, there are also scammers and con artists
inside prison; inmates are going to zero in on me right away.

I'm duly tentative. I excuse myself and slip into a bathroom, closing the door behind me. I get on my knees, and
I pray to God. I still don't know if anyone is listening. But
I pray anyway, hoping I won't be the effectively functionless idiot I am.

I shouldn't be nervous, even though I am. I need to push aside my own problems. They're still back there in Illinois. Nothing's been resolved. I'm still ruined. The university process isn't over yet. I didn't expect to be back in Oklahoma so soon. But here I am. In cowboy boots, this time. And this, I remind myself, isn't about me. This is about them, the inmates. No time for jitters. I pray I will have the strength to be peaceful, to be helpful to the prisoners.

Rhonda's right. After I remove myself from the bathroom, even before I get to the podium, several prisoners converge. I'm hearing names, DOC numbers, rushed stories of convictions based on bad information, of excessive sentences, of lives crushed. I'm taking notes. I can feel the quiet desperation. They want an address to write to us at Another Chance Justice Project. To contact us for help. Because they have nothing else. No one else. Because they are out of options to get out of here. I'm giving out our address. But now it's time.

Eric and I stand before about two hundred women seated in an auditorium. This was Eric's idea. It was born of failure. While we were just able to help seven of nine women gain their freedom through parole, the two who didn't make it got Eric thinking. What if we could try to prevent that from happening again? What if we could create a program to better educate inmates and their families about the parole process, to avoid the pitfalls that resulted in those two inmates losing their chance at freedom? To wit: Don't get in trouble. Avoid misconducts in prison.

But it was more than that. I'd learned, in speaking with inmates, they often didn't know the basics, that they could write a letter on their own behalf to the parole board. They could explain how they changed, how they had a plan of action once they were released. I'd also learned, in speaking with their families, they too were often in the dark. They didn't know their loved ones were about to come up for parole. They didn't know they could write letters of support. Neither did they know what to say in those letters. They didn't know they could show up at the nearly barren parole board meeting in Oklahoma City.

So I put together a pre-parole presentation. I had little idea, incidentally, what I was doing, so it was a good thing I had the help of Lynn, my unofficial expert in the parole process, who devoted so much of her life trying to help her ex-husband gain his freedom after being convicted of murder. Lynn edited my presentation, which gave me the confidence to try something I should have known would be ridiculed.

At the end of the presentation, I created a "Certificate of Completion." I used fancy fonts. Every inmate who sat (suffered) through my pre-parole presentation would receive a certificate, which they could put in their file. And that certificate, in turn, could be one more factoid to present to the parole board in their bid to gain their freedom.

But as Eric spoke first, I stood next to him at the

podium, looking at a sea of expectant faces, and suddenly, I felt a cold shiver of realization: What was I thinking? The idea for the certificate came to me late at night, when I should have known better, when I should have left well enough alone and gone to bed before causing more damage. After all, who was I to concoct a certificate of any kind? It's not like I was authorized. There was nothing official about it. Nobody licensed it. The certificate was an illusion, from my brain to my laptop to a printer.

But flash forward, here I was, and out of the corner of my eye, I caught a hardened stare from an elderly inmate sitting up front not two feet from me.

She appeared unalterably, unblinkingly angry. At me. Even though I hadn't spoken a word yet. She looked like I had already offended her. Eyes narrowed. Mouth set. Mirthless. I would have stepped over and apologized for my general existence, but Eric finished speaking, and it was my turn.

I had a presentation to present. So I started jabbering on. And while I jabbered, a second track in my mind was having its own internal dialogue, telling me what I was saying out loud to an auditorium packed full of prisoners was ridiculously rudimentary. Of course they should stay out of trouble. They know that. They don't need to hear you say that, numbskull. Okay, genius, now what are you going to tell them? That they shouldn't have gotten in trouble in the first place? Goodness gracious. You know who must think you're an epic idiot? That elderly inmate right up front. So I catch a glimpse of her, and I'm stunned. She's weeping quietly. The tears are coming down. She's almost smiling. I'm not sure why but I keep talking because I'm up at the podium in front of two hundred inmates, and that's what you're supposed to do when you're up at the podium in front of two hundred inmates.

Finally, I shut up because my time is up. Conveniently, I don't mention anything about my utterly absurd certificates of completion. I think I'm in the clear, scot-free, when I hear Rhonda, my colleague, in the back of the auditorium call out to the throng of inmates that there's a certificate of completion for each and every one of them! I'm about to cringe. But I don't have time. There's an eruption from the audience, a thunderous whooping it up.

The inmates are elated. I'm flummoxed. Then nearly happy. Until I'm not. Because now I'm nearly sad. Or maybe both. I'm not sure why. I can't quite articulate the swing in emotion until I reflect on it later. I was genuinely glad the prisoners were happy, but it made me sad that all it took was a piece of paper to make them happy. Because they were largely forgotten. Because they were without. Whether they were innocent or guilty, they were suffering greatly. They were someone's daughter. They were someone's sister. They were someone's mother. They were someone.

I was ashamed of myself. For being so obtuse. For not getting it. For not understanding their loss. Along with Eric,

I left prison that day suddenly appreciating that, if I wanted, I could walk into a convenience store and buy a candy bar. No one would stop me. I didn't need to ask for permission. I wasn't under lock and key. That candy bar was just there for the taking. Not that I ever did. But I was beginning to feel not entirely essentially functionless.

In short order, dozens of women gained their freedom through parole. Prison gates began to open all over the place in the coming days. Not just in Oklahoma. But in other parts of the country, too.

Before long, a Florida judge vacated the murder conviction of a Miami man named Tony Brown, also known as Andre Gonzales, who had been sentenced to life in prison. I investigated that case with my students a few years earlier.

We were trying to track down a potential witness to a murder, a club bouncer who was only known as "Maniac." We didn't know his real name. We had nothing else to go on. Maniac earned the nickname. Big, tough guy who, when the mood struck him, put his large fist into some people's faces. Authorities never found him. There were, as it turns out, a lot of Maniacs out there. But I taught my students how to track down elusive sources and gave them access to proprietary databases that know practically everything, including maybe your horoscope.

One source led to another, and my students located a particularly promising Maniac who was in a Florida prison on an unrelated charge. We weren't sure he was the right

Maniac. Actually, we had little more than a hunch. I figured there was one way to find out. Can't succeed, I say, unless you're willing to fail. So I flew down to Florida with a group of students.

We met Maniac at a spartan cafeteria table where he was incarcerated. He proceeded to tell us he hadn't known anyone was arrested, let alone sentenced to life in prison, for the murder in question until we contacted him by mail. Indeed, he didn't know Tony Brown, a.k.a. Andre Gonzales. What Maniac did know was they got the wrong guy. Because Maniac knew who committed the murder. Because he witnessed it. But he never said anything about it. He called it the "code of silence."

In this rough-hewn neighborhood, you kept your mouth shut or you ended up silenced for good. Sitting at the barren prison cafeteria, I was stunned so much, the questions tumbled out of my mouth in rushed disarray. We suddenly had it on good authority that Andre was wrongfully convicted. It was also one of those moments when you realize at a deeper level the world is sometimes awry. This actually happens. People are falsely accused. They are mistakenly punished for wrongs they didn't commit. If you are a black man in America, like Andre, you are at greater risk of being incarcerated—and wrongfully convicted, studies show. This all happens under the mantle of what many consider the best, most advanced system of justice in the world, honed after centuries, based on the scholarship of great minds, after the workings of highly trained lawyers sparring in a carefully choreographed courtroom.

None of that mattered at the moment. Maniac was on tape. We rushed back to Illinois to write and publish the story of our findings. Then waited. And waited. Until a few years later. After being sentenced to life in prison for a crime he didn't commit, Andre's conviction was vacated after spending twelve years in prison, and the prosecution declined to retry him. Andre was free. Finally. It made national news. University officials who had nothing to do with it intoned about the great investigative journalism that set Andre free. I was erased from the narrative. It was okay. Because Andre was *free*. That was the thing. That was what mattered.

A lifetime in prison, gone. Unshackled from a wrongful conviction. In its own way, Andre's freedom lightened my own sense of burden, of ruin, especially when I heard from a former student who fondly remembered the experience as we hunted for the truth, and when I heard from a key player in the legal proceedings who wrote a private note.

It is no exaggeration that Mr. Brown's release is due in no small part to your program's efforts. I'm sure most, if not all, the original students who worked on the report have graduated. I hope you are able to convey to them the pivotal role they played in ensuring our judicial system upholds its promise of providing justice to all.

Consider it conveyed. But I'm getting ahead of myself. It was almost strange. These things didn't happen. People weren't just set free from life sentences for murder. And yet, in the coming months, I kept feeling the reverberations, how the unseen forces of justice were beginning to prevail.

Around the time Andre was set free in Miami, Florida, a higher force was at work in Cook County, Illinois. The top prosecutor there made a remarkable public pronouncement: She was backing the clemency of Ysole Krol, who had already served seven years of a thirty-five-year sentence after being convicted of first-degree murder.

I had investigated that shooting with my students a couple of years earlier. And here's what we found: Ysole hadn't pulled the trigger. In fact, it was unclear whether Ysole, sitting in the passenger seat of a car, even touched the gun in the glove compartment before her then-boyfriend yelled at her to open it, and he grabbed the weapon and fired it at a group of boys attacking them. It was certainly in doubt whether Ysole knew what the boyfriend was going to do, whether she could read his mind, whether she thought he was going to just brandish the gun to ward off the group of assailants, or whether he intended to pull the trigger.

But this much was certain: Ysole, then a teenager, was torn from her young daughter in the aftermath of that split second, when everything in her life changed, and she was sentenced. Over-sentenced, in my opinion. Now, the state's attorney, the county's elected prosecutor, was of the same mind. Suddenly, it appeared Ysole might gain her freedom. Same for Amber Kirk. Another strange occurrence, by the by. I had heard about Amber's case many months earlier. She was sentenced to life in prison in Oklahoma. Incarcerated on a road called Kickapoo I'd get to know later. And yet she hadn't killed anyone. She hadn't maimed anyone, except herself, in a way. A nonviolent offender, she was put in prison for life after failing drug court, an alternative to hard time in prison.

I knew of convicted killers who got far less than life— maybe twenty years—for murder. Amber? She was a drug addict who relapsed. But did I hear that right? Yes, she was locked up for life on drug charges.

So I sent a reporter from Illinois to document this story in Oklahoma. This, incidentally, was a little before my own troubles, before I was recruited to Oklahoma to help inmates there. This was when I was still running The Medill Justice Project. That Amber's case was several states away in Oklahoma mattered not at all to me. We went wherever the injustice was. And this, in my estimation, was a gross injustice.

Amber's story, however, ostensibly died when I was destroyed. The reporter dropped the assignment after I went on administrative leave from the university. That was the end of it. Or at least that's what I thought.

Months later, when I traveled from Illinois to Oklahoma, lost in my own misery, I found Amber again. It wasn't simply that she was still locked up. It was that she found me without realizing it. She wrote to our fledgling nonprofit, Another Chance Justice Project, without knowing I was there. All she knew was she needed help.

I instantly recognized Amber's name when I read her letter. I also instantly decided we'd help her. But what I didn't instantly get was it was an odd happenstance. I was drawn to her case before, and here I was returning to it. There was no apparent reason I'd be connected to Amber's case again, from the time I encountered her when I was in Illinois to bumping into her again when I was in Oklahoma. A coincidence? Divine intervention? If so, I didn't get it because I wasn't exactly paying attention.

Because I didn't get another thing: Commutation. That's what Amber was seeking. But what was commutation? I mean, I had a general idea that commutations had to do with inmates trying to seek clemency, either in the form of a reduced sentence or through their release from prison altogether.

But that wasn't nearly enough. The first thing I needed to do was figure out exactly how it worked. I needed to learn much more if I was to be helpful to Amber, to help set her free. So I returned to DeLynn, the head of the parole board. I asked her more dumb questions. I think she expected them when she heard from me. She answered them with the same aplomb and patience as before. And my research yielded this fact: Amber had almost no chance of gaining her freedom.

Well, okay. There were other facts. For one, seeking commutation was sort of like playing the lottery. Big if you win. But statistically far-fetched. Especially here in Oklahoma, where the decision makers were those same five folks, they of the hardline: the Pardon and Parole Board. Now, this wasn't parole we were talking about, which, by comparison, almost seemed like child's play, given how much easier it was to grasp. Prisoners automatically find themselves on the parole docket once a year—some must wait longer, depending on the nature of the crime—and then there's a vote. With commutation, there were so many other variables.

For one, prisoners could submit their first commutation application at any time, which raised the natural question: When should that be? The answer to that question was intertwined with so many other questions, such as: Who was on the parole board, when would they step down, and who would replace them?

Complicating matters was the commutation application. A hefty eighteen pages. Then revised upward to nineteen pages. Packed with a dizzying array of questions. They wanted to know just about everything. They wanted a detailed accounting of each offense. They even wanted to know about the offenses for which the inmate wasn't charged.

And then there was this: The process was multi-layered. For the first stage, the parole board would consider your commutation on paper, meaning they'd consider your application and, in your absence, vote. This was known as a qualification review, which, as I learned, was a long-shot gauntlet. Hard to impossible to get through with the necessary three-vote majority of the five-member parole board. If you survived that, you moved onto the second stage, some months later, after the parole board vetted your case with the help of an internal investigator, to learn everything there was to know about you and the extent to which you were a troublemaker and a risk to society. This stage was known as a personal appearance. Except that is a bit of a misnomer because it didn't feel terribly personal. What was likely was, you'd be beamed in via video conferencing from prison, staring at a lineup of stern-looking parole board members back in that cavernous room in Oklahoma City. You'd get a handful of minutes to tell your story. They'd probably ask you some tough questions, some of which might be akin to: Why should we give you a second chance?

You'd also get what were known as "delegates," two of whom would be allowed to sit with you, one of whom would be allowed a hundred and twenty seconds to speak to help save your life from prison. If you survived that second round, which also was pretty darn unlikely, you'd sit and wait for an indeterminate amount of time for the judgment of the governor, then a hardliner herself, who had the final word about whether your life would be saved and you'd be granted your freedom.

Whew.

There will be a test on that later. Actually, the real test was to get beyond the facts and figures populating that voluminous commutation application. To tell the human story. To show the nuanced picture of this person. It wasn't simply that Amber was convicted of "manufacturing" meth. It was that such a description didn't fit the crime.

As it happened, Amber was once asleep on a couch in a busted-up trailer at the end of a country dirt road without a street name. That's when authorities barged in, and Amber instinctively ran for it, bolting out of a window. What was found behind were some of the basic ingredients to make meth. Not what I'd consider "manufacturing." Amber was no drug overlord.

She was sentenced like one nonetheless. Life is a lot. Especially in prison. Especially if you've never been accused of causing violence on another. There were, as I quickly learned, others like Amber, overpopulating overcrowded prisons costing Oklahoma taxpayers millions. Sheila Royal, for one. She was suffering from major illnesses, which necessitated the amputation of part of a foot. She too was given life for selling drugs. I helped her with her commutation application.

Another inmate, Robyn Allen, was also struggling with physical disabilities, desperately trying to put food on the table for her children when she sold small amounts of dope out of a house. She readily admits it. She also readily got twenty years in prison for it. I helped Robyn with her commutation application.

And then there was Kelsey Dodson. Of all the letters piling up at our little nonprofit, there was something about what she handwrote about her tragic story that instantly resonated with me.

Kelsey was a young mother of twenty when, late one night, her infant daughter began to exhibit symptoms of distress, including vomiting.

When her daughter's eyes stopped tracking Kelsey's finger, she did what any mother would do, which was to rush her daughter to the ER in the middle of the night. Her then live-in boyfriend told Kelsey he wasn't coming along. "What if we are accused of child abuse?" he asked.

The next thing Kelsey knew, she was being accused of having hurt her own child. The boyfriend, a known small-time drug dealer, wasn't charged with anything, though he'd been watching the child alone at home in the hours prior to her medical collapse.

That night, Kelsey was at work, making sandwiches at a nearby Subway shop, before she returned home and soon found their child unresponsive. The boyfriend went on to leave a litter of crimes in his wake in the ensuing years, including arson, records showed. Kelsey went on to face a legal nightmare.

Maintaining her innocence all along, Kelsey was acquitted of child abuse, the main charge. But the jury found her guilty of child neglect, which, based on my reading of the trial transcript, meant jurors determined Kelsey didn't act fast enough to take her daughter to the ER. And yet it appeared to me, after reviewing records and conducting interviews, that had Kelsey not acted as soon as she did, her daughter might not be alive today. Kelsey may have saved her child's life. The jury never learned this essential fact: what happened to Kelsey's daughter. That she survived. That Kelsey's daughter is thriving today. A happy little girl, she plays with her iPad. She jumps in the pool. She just doesn't know her mother.

Because Kelsey got twenty years.

By the time I spoke with Kelsey, she'd been incarcerated for about eight years, which in prison time is more like eighty years.

My thinking: There's not much humanity in prison. Except in Kelsey's case, there was something off. Even by phone, I could sense it. There was an innocence there. A softness. Kelsey somehow retained who she was. Kelsey was someone who hadn't become hardened by the hard time. I met her mother, stepfather, and sister. Good people. Kelsey didn't have a long rap sheet. She stayed to herself and out of trouble in prison, with the exception of some minor infractions. The Good Housekeeping Stamp of Approval came from an unsolicited remark of Rhonda, my colleague at Another Chance Justice Project, who was in and out of prisons every week, helping inmates through her program, Women in Transition. Kelsey, she said, was good.

It just so happened I knew a lot about Kelsey's case even before I knew it. I spent years investigating matters just like hers. They are called shaken-baby syndrome cases. The dynamics: An infant becomes unresponsive. The symptoms are largely internal head injuries, a triad of brain bleeding, brain swelling, and bleeding within the eyes.

But often there is no physical evidence the accused—typically a mother—did anything to hurt the infant. There are no witnesses alleging a crime occurred. There may have been no crime. An infant can't speak, so it's left to doctors and crime solvers to try to figure out what happened. Over the years, there's been a growing debate in the medical community about how to diagnose shaken-baby syndrome. The orthodoxy has been challenged. Indeed, medical experts have come to understand the same symptoms associated with shaken-baby syndrome can be the result of a newborn passing through the narrow birth canal, or congenital medical conditions, or rare illnesses, or even short falls. None of which, by the way, are crimes.

Even if a crime did occur, experts have come to realize over the years there's a real question about whether the perpetrator can be identified. Studies have shown there's something called a "lucid interval." It's a fancy way of saying an infant can sustain an internal head injury but appear to be fine for hours or days before collapsing into a medical emergency.

So how do we know exactly when the child was injured

and by whom—if anyone—especially when the infant can't tell us what happened and there are no witnesses, except the accused?

Years ago, when I decided we at The Medill Justice Project would investigate shaken-baby syndrome cases, I asked my students to locate the father of the diagnosis, a pediatric neurosurgeon named Norman Guthkelch.

I figured he could give us insight into the origins. What I didn't figure was this: Norman lived about three miles away from the Illinois campus, of all places, in a quaint retirement home. What were the chances? I mean, he was from over the pond in Great Britain. He had that cool clipped accent that made the English language sound better. But what was he doing in my proverbial backyard? I dismissed the astronomical unlikelihood.

I also gave little thought when we met Norman, the gentleman, and he alluded to a vision earlier in his career. I gently probed. He reluctantly revealed. He saw Jesus in person. I asked more. I wanted to know more. I mean, here was a highly educated retired neurosurgeon, a man of science, who lived for nearly a century. There must be great wisdom in the depth of his experience. What was it all about? God is love. That's what he said. But not much more. Norman was a bit cryptic; he feared people would react badly to it. In this day and age, such things are scoffed at, and it could call into question everything else about the man.

You'd think I'd scoff, too. I was, as might be recalled,

a non-believing heathen. But I didn't. For some reason I can't fully account for, my feeling at that moment was, as a journalist, who was I to discard the authenticity of what I haven't inspected, what I haven't investigated, what I don't understand?

Heck, I've always been stuck on the idea we can't comprehend infinity, or even more to the point: What happens when you go straight up, like a rocket, past the skies, into space, beyond the galaxies? We can't comprehend what's outside the outer limit. I mean, what's after *after?* This, though, I comprehended: The father of shaken-baby syndrome, he who wrote the seminal medical paper in 1971, questioned his own diagnosis.

He said, in no uncertain terms, innocent people were being accused and convicted of crimes they didn't commit. He was sure of it. Nearly a hundred years old, he was still at work, dissecting a stack of cases on his desk in this retirement home close to campus because he wanted to get to the bottom of them all.

I'll never forget what he said, not long before he passed away, that doctors were trained to heal, not to detect crimes. And yet, in the years after the establishment of shaken-baby syndrome as a diagnosis, that's precisely what was happening. Doctors were treating infants, identifying what they believed to be crimes, notifying police, which in turn cuffed people who were sent away.

In Kelsey's case, police made a basic assumption based

on what she and the boyfriend said and what doctors at the hospital told them: The child cried out while Kelsey was attending to her. Thus, authorities made a leaping assumption, concluding Kelsey must have hurt her child. Because the mother was in proximity in time and place to the daughter when the daughter cried out. That's what the trial transcript showed, a stunning lack of nuance.

$A + B = C.$

My own diagnosis: This wasn't addition. This was algebra. There was a missing variable in the equation. That the child could have cried out *not* because her mother caused her harm. Rather, the child cried out after the lucid interval, *after* the buildup of whatever was happening inside of her little head, when the medical emergency finally arrived.

Kelsey, unfortunately, didn't have an x-ray machine in her modest apartment. Or a computed tomography scanner. Or a magnetic resonance imaging chamber. Because those hugely expensive hospital contraptions were about the only things that could have helped her see what the naked eye couldn't. I was determined to help Kelsey with her commutation application.

I was also determined to help Lisa Rae Moss. This one was different. I didn't pick her case. It chose me. We received word from Lisa Rae's friends in Florida. They wanted us to take a look at her case. To see if there was anything we could do. Strangely enough, I also instantly remembered Lisa Rae's letter among the droves coming in.

Her case was pretty cut and dried—at least at a first glance. Lisa Rae plotted to have someone kill her husband. And that's what happened. Lisa Rae's brother shot her husband dead. But the more I looked into the case seeking clarity, the more I found it clouded with opacity.

Lisa Rae testified she was abused repeatedly by her husband. He drew a weapon on her. She was fearful for her life.

Why didn't you go to police? I asked her.

"A piece of paper wouldn't have saved me," she told me.

A piece of paper. I understood the implication, an order of protection wouldn't have shielded Lisa Rae from her husband's rage. Especially in their small town in Oklahoma. Especially back then, some thirty years earlier, when this happened.

Battered Wife Syndrome hadn't emerged yet as a viable defense for women who faced imminent physical threat to life and limb from their abusive husbands. Lisa Rae received life without the possibility of parole for her crime. So did her brother. Since her sentencing, other women battered by their husbands had, in some cases, received far less punishment. One got about seven years.

Lisa Rae didn't have the benefit of timing. Or maybe she did. Because she did her time finding herself. Who she found was God.

From a twenty-something-year-old wife and mother, Lisa Rae, over three decades of imprisonment, became a mature person of faith. Her devotion led her to take a course in prison on faith. Then she launched her own prison ministry, A Queen's Heart, based on a small Bible study group.

Lisa Rae accepted responsibility for her role in what happened all those years before. She accepted the weight of time, the unrelenting year after year of prison, with only more time lapping by her.

When we spoke by phone, she often referenced Scripture. But they weren't just words. It's what sustained her, kept her going, propelled her forward in hope when there appeared none.

That's when something began to dawn on me. God's presence could be found in prisons, too. Faith was sometimes never more powerful than among those without. Without family. Without their sons and daughters. Without money and careers and cars and the other mundane trappings of life. When all was lost. When it seemed it was all over. Lives of unspeakable suffering. That's where I'd see the manifestations of God. Behind barbed wire. Where you couldn't escape. I'd see an inmate swaying, eyes tightly shut, tattooed arms raised to heaven, taking in the mellifluous sound of church music piped into a prison chapel, taking no heed of all of those around her, living in a different existence, on a different plane, that couldn't be seen or taken away.

That's when I also met Stacie. She was a friend of Lisa Rae's on the outside, part of the group of friends who wanted to see if there was something we could do to help such a transformed inmate.

When I first called Stacie, it was to find out more about Lisa Rae and her case. Stacie had other ideas. She first wanted to find out about me. I tried to brush it off, giving her a pat answer, telling her little about me, particularly not about my general state of disgrace. But she wouldn't have it. I think she sensed something else there, even though I hadn't revealed much more than my first name.

Indeed, I'd gotten in the habit of giving out little more than my given name while investigating cases in Oklahoma because (1) nobody seemed to really care who I was as long as I was there to help their loved ones, and (2) I was ruined, and I didn't want that to detract from me helping their loved ones.

Stacie, though, was waiting for a real answer. I'm not sure why, but I instantly decided to give her one. I felt myself letting go. Okay. Here goes. Headlong into the abyss. I told her everything. Not just my background as an investigative reporter at the *Washington Post*. Not just my years investigating wrongful convictions. But the rest of the whole messy lot, the false accusations, and the destruction.

I was wincing when I was done explaining, one eye closed, waiting for Stacie to hang up, anticipating the dead dial tone, expecting the judgment and the ire. There was none. What there was, was compassion. Stacie had this almost otherworldly way of understanding more than what I said, or the convoluted way I said it.

It felt as if she expected this unrevealed story to reveal

itself; this was who I was going to be before I told her who I was.

I should have known. Stacie was a believer. More. She was imbued with powerful messages of God. Stacie told me this is what happens when you are on the battlefield for Christ. She told me this is what happens when you fight for the wrongfully convicted, for those in prison suffering. She told me the enemy will steal, kill, and destroy. I didn't know what to say. I didn't know about any battlefield for Christ. I only knew I was overcome with emotion. Good thing Stacie couldn't see me on the other end of the line. She asked if she could make a prayer. I said yes and closed my eyes as she spoke a steady stream of Scripture for several uninterrupted minutes, the net of which felt like a force of winds billowing my sails. I almost felt a kernel of hope.

I'll say this. I've never had a first telephone conversation with a stranger like that. Where I revealed my terrible situation. Where I was overcome with emotion. And I prayed. But there was nothing ordinary about Stacie.

Later, she sent me this email: "Hi Alec, I believe without doubt that God has an amazing plan for your life beyond these present circumstances. I also believe He has connected the two of us 'for such a time as this' so that I may be an encouragement to you as you grow in your faith, as others were to me when I was new to my faith. I want to share this passage in the book of Hebrews (Amplified Bible) that reads as if it were written for you only:

But be ever mindful of the days gone by in which, after you were spiritually enlightened, you endured a great and painful struggle,

Sometimes being yourselves a gazingstock, publicly exposed to insults and abuse and distress, and sometimes claiming fellowship and making common cause with others who were so treated.

For you did sympathize and suffer along with those who were imprisoned, and you bore cheerfully the plundering of your belongings and the confiscation of your property, in the knowledge and consciousness that you yourselves had a better and lasting possession.

Do not, therefore, fling away your fearless confidence, for it carries a great and glorious compensation of reward.

For you have need of steadfast patience and endurance, so that you may perform and fully accomplish the will of God, and thus receive and carry away [and enjoy to the full] what is promised.

For still a little while (a very little while), and the Coming One will come and He will not delay.

But the just shall live by faith [My righteous servant shall live by his conviction respecting man's relationship to God and divine things, and holy fervor born of faith and conjoined with it]; (Hebrews 10:32–38 AMP).

I sat there thinking: Exactly. Years earlier, when I was introduced to that book about Jesus, it felt like a "spiritual enlightening"—it certainly got me thinking, altered my mind-set.

Then, I'd say, I "endured a great and painful struggle." I was also "publicly exposed to insults and abuse and distress." And I "did sympathize and suffer along with those who were imprisoned," especially those inmates I tried to help win their freedom.

The only thing is, I'm not sure I "cheerfully" bore the subsequent "plundering." Maybe "quietly." Or "stoically." But let's not quibble over semantics.

There was this, too: My suffering, strangely enough, wasn't pulling me away from faith; it wasn't causing me to blame God—or anyone else—for my misfortune. Rather, my suffering was drawing me closer to a deeper sense of faith.

The more pain I felt, and it was constant, the more I sought solace in a higher power.

The more I felt utterly lost in a ferocious hurricane that never seemed to want to end, the more I grasped for strength in an unseen force.

When there was no peace, I found comfort in a search for faith, for meaning when nothing made sense, when I was suffocating on myself.

Maybe I just didn't know where else to turn. Maybe the meds were indeed altering my brain chemistry. Maybe I was just losing my mind. But this was an unalterable fact:

It began to occur to me that nearly everyone I was encountering at this inflection point in my life—when I didn't think I was going to make it—was a follower of Jesus, a devout believer in Christ.

Not just my old friend, Kevin, he of the Jesus book, with whom I started attending Life.Church when I was in town. I discovered comfort in the sermons of Senior Pastor Craig Groeschel. He was funny. He was smart. He was compelling. His messages were of goodness, of kindness, of the way Jesus spread the Gospel before the world.

There was nothing odd, off-putting, or freakish about any of it, the message, or the messenger. Okay. Two things. Pastor Groeschel was remote. I mean, not distant, as in cold. But as in, he was far away. Pastor Groeschel was beamed into the church auditorium by video on a movie-sized screen. Turned out, Pastor Groeschel, the founder of Life. Church, has a massive following across multiple states. He couldn't be in all places all the time. I couldn't hold that against him. Pastor Groeschel also has pretty big biceps for a man of faith. But, hey, who said pastors couldn't have big biceps? I couldn't hold that against him, either.

I also found comfort in my friend Rhonda, who openly prayed over large and small matters, so great was her beautiful faith. That included when I helped move a monstrously sized television set up a tight turn of stairs in the home of Michelle Murphy, a mournful soul who endured nearly two decades in prison for a horrific crime she didn't commit before being exonerated.

I felt comfort in Kathy, too, who prayed to Jesus with me in the parole parking lot.

There was also Kate Parker, a great person of faith who was nowhere near Tulsa, just in case it seemed like a geographic thing. Because it wasn't. Because Kate, a true believer, was all the way on the West Coast.

I helped Kate gain her freedom after she was wrongfully accused of abuse. She reached out to see if I was okay. She told me she and her family had my back. She wanted to fight the good fight, going public with her support for me. I made sure she didn't. It would not redound in a good way on her. She went ahead, privately sending a fierce letter to the university, testifying to my character and knowledge about me as a person and professor.

There were several other followers of Jesus, Josonda, and all the others I kept bumping into almost daily, who embraced me, in such a concentrated period, it almost felt—I'm not sure I can phrase it any other way—I was being encircled by followers of Christ.

That included Stacie. She happened to live in Florida, by the way. So this phenomenon, if I might call it that, of being embraced by followers of Jesus, was happening coast to coast and in between.

To this point, I'd been largely self-taught when it came to the Bible. I read it on my own. I read books about Jesus. But now, I felt like I was receiving tutelage. Stacie talked about intercessions—prayers on behalf of another—and prayer warriors, of which she was a mighty one. Stacie told me she'd pray for me as would her group of fellow prayer warriors. I was surprised, given the skeptic I was, how much this brought comfort.

The effect, as it turned out, was immediate. I suddenly felt peace even while I remained dangling in an as-yet unresolved university matter. I suddenly didn't worry about more negative press looming over me. I could see Julie-Ann's occasional fury for what it was, overwhelming fear and anxiety over the uncertainty for our family, the destruction of our lives, the end of our marriage, the imminent threat to our home and livelihood. I suddenly didn't feel anger when she laid into me. I suddenly didn't respond the way I might have before. I suddenly didn't return fire with fire. I suddenly didn't say things I would regret later. I felt compassion. I was almost surprised by my own transformation. I could *almost* feel Jesus gently resting a hand on my right shoulder, helping me to be still, to be calm in the storm, whatever came my way. I know some people will think it's crazy. Maybe it was. Maybe I was just imagining things. Maybe I just reached the breaking point.

I'm not sure I would have survived otherwise. I'm not sure what I would have done to myself, had it not been for the sudden appearance, out of literally nowhere, of a phalanx of followers of Christ.

I felt, well, saved.

At about the same time, I found comfort from another unlikely source: Eli and Brody. Two more dogs. On my latest trip to Tulsa, I dog-sat for my friend Kevin's older daughter and husband who were on vacation. At first, I had trouble telling Eli and Brody apart, they looked so similar: scruffy, slightly grouchy, and fluffy white. By the end of my stay, though, I could recognize their distinct personalities, one more docile than the other, one a real cuddler, the other more of a roughhouser. We'd become great friends. This was no doubt owing to my penchant to produce high-end treats. But that was okay with me. It was a small price to pay for what they gave to me when I needed it most.

chapter nine

I'm sitting in an Uber. I'm a customer, but I'm imagining what it's like up in front of the dashboard, in the driver's seat. I'm still thinking about the potential for this line of work, Ubering, because what else can I do, when my career has been foreclosed, when the entire fields of education and journalism are out the window—the only things I know— heck, when I can't work among other people, in an office, any office, after all the accusations?

I'm still, technically speaking, a full, tenured professor, but that feels like semantics. I've always been something of a realist. I'm already ruined in the court of public opinion, in the media, and I can see where this is all heading. I can't envision a scenario where I'd return to the university, no matter the ultimate outcome of its investigation. I don't want to go back. Actually, I don't want to ever teach again. I don't have the heart for it anymore. Granted, I don't have the heart to do much of anything when I'm not helping inmates.

But. I could drive. I could navigate down winding roads at the wheel of a vehicle. Hence, I'm quizzing my Uber driver about the particulars of the job. We're going over hours. Bathroom breaks. Potential daily income. Minus gas. Mileage. Everything's going fine until we get to qualifications. Then we come to a screeching halt.

Caught in midtown traffic. My car is too old. Way too old. Seventeen years old. Can't drive customers around in a clunker. What about leasing a new car? Nyet. There are limitations on the miles you're allowed to drive a leased car in a given year, and it's not nearly enough for an Uber professional. What about buying a new car? Oh, sure, spend tens of thousands of dollars to make, say, fifteen dollars an hour. No logic to that. Maybe trade in the old clunker, which is worth about two dollars, for a used car that isn't too used and isn't too expensive. I do a quick search on my iPhone. I'm appalled by the steep prices of used cars. Who in the world is buying this stuff? Not me. The interrogatory is over. So is my Uber career before it started.

We arrive at my destination, I thank the driver and step

out into the light. A moment later, an Uber prompt pops up on my smartphone, asking me to rate my trip: "How was your Monday morning trip with jesus?"

I do a double take. Jesus? Then I rationalize. There are plenty of people named Jesus. They could certainly be Uber drivers. And let's not overlook the tiny fact the "j" in "Jesus" was not capitalized in the Uber prompt. So there. No reason to get carried away.

But then New York City assaults the senses. Blaring horns. The pervasive stench of urine. Droves of stern-faced people barreling by.

Bedlam. Just like I remember it. Like it's always been. Once upon a time, I thought everyone lived like this, crowded like canned sardines on a rickety subway rumbling to school. I thought everyone spoke with a New York accent. I taught my daughter the street lexicon: "Whassa matta for you?" And my other New York favorite: "You talkin' to me? You talkin' to *me?* Cuz I don't see nobody else." My daughter got the accent down. Now I'm a schlub from a faceless suburb that aspires to be its tidy self.

I've been ushered out the door of my own home, coaxed from the catatonia of the Chicago suburbs to my natural habitat, the island of Manhattan, to be with family. Come home, my sisters say. Stay awhile, my mother says. We'll feed you, they say. They've heard my face has been planted in a rug. They're concerned.

I peer around, get the lay of the land. I gaze at a falafel

place. Used to be a barber's when I was a kid. Mr. Kay's. He'd cut my hair, half paying attention while talking to guys sitting in chairs doing nothing but smoking cigars. Across the street, an upscale pharmacy. I walk over. Go to the counter. I tell the clerk this used to be a hole-in-the-wall convenience store. Offended, he tells me, no, no, it's always been a pharmacy. Not a million years ago, I say. It used to be Mr. Lee's. I'd walk home up Broadway instead of taking the public bus, to save the fare, all of twenty-five cents. That way, I could burrow down the crowded aisles of Mr. Lee's narrow little store to buy really important stuff, like baseball cards, comic books, and chewing gum. Mr. Lee would cut me a break if I didn't have enough change on me.

Another odd occurrence. I'm staying with my sister Kathy, her husband, Adam, and their adorable infant daughter, who happen to live around the corner from where Mr. Lee's used to be, in the apartment building right next to the one where I lived for many years of my childhood. In New York City, there's roughly a gazillion apartment buildings. So this is totally random. Or not?

If not, I'm unaware of the significance. All I sense is the distant echo of Mary, hollering at me—the eight-year-old version of me—as I ran up 104th Street. Mary. Good old Mary. After my mother lost custody of my sister and me, we went to live with my father here on the Upper West Side for a time.

Mary was my father's nanny when he was a little runt

growing up in Yonkers, on the outskirts of New York. Mary would cover for him when he didn't practice the accordion like he was supposed to. Later, when my father grew up, while he worked long hours at the *New York Times*, Mary, like a mother, looked after Karen and me. *Mary.* Rest her soul.

New York does that to me, brings me back to times before. That's why I'm barely paying attention later in the day, at Han Dynasty, a Chinese restaurant where I'm seated next to my little Japanese mother. I'm not saying anything because I have nothing to say and I don't want to be here, not because I don't *really* want to be here, but because I can't process the idea of small talk, of socializing for the sake of socializing, when I feel little but despair, so all I can do is wait until the meal is mercifully over.

But in the meanwhile, my mother is chatting with my sisters Karen and Kathy and Kathy's husband, Adam, about who knows what. Kathy and Adam's little girl alertly glances at her mommy and daddy and then, from her perch in a high chair, flings perfectly good fried rice onto the floor, exceedingly delighted by the results.

Modern art.

I'm mildly entertained, too. I wouldn't mind flinging my own fried rice on the floor without any consequence from time to time.

There's a wonderful purity in Kathy's child, not yet a year old. An innocence. A blank slate. It's all before her, the whole messy kit and caboodle. I want to have a serious conversation with her. Schedule a meeting with the tyke. Tell her about the pitfalls. Shield her from the hurts. Protect her from the insanity of it all. So she doesn't end up like me, damaged goods.

She can't read yet, so I haven't sent her a copy of *The Case for Christ*. But I've sent copies of the book to a bunch of literate people. To my in-laws, who've stood by me, unwavering in their love and support, throughout the ordeal with the university. To friends. To every member of my immediate family. None around the table at the Chinese restaurant has read it. Because everyone thinks I'm nuts.

Okay. Let me unpack that. It's true, the only thing I read these days is about God. I can't read a book otherwise. It just can't hold my attention. It doesn't compute. It's just a collection of characters comprising words filling a page.

After dinner, my sister Kathy and I sit at her dining room table talking about God late into the evening. Well, that's what I talk about. Kathy, raised a Baptist, married into a devout family of believers, including her husband, Adam, a great guy, so she doesn't completely tune me out.

I'm talking about the biblical story of Joseph, which I've just read for the first time. It was quite a revelation for me, coming so late to the game, not even knowing the commercialized Broadway version of *Joseph and the Amazing Technicolor Dreamcoat*. Yes, I grew up kind of in a closet.

In that closet, Joseph never came up. So here I was,

finally getting around to reading the Bible, when I couldn't believe this elaborate, page-turner of a story about a guy named Joseph who was betrayed by his jealous brothers, sold into slavery, falsely accused of sexual misconduct, and wrongfully imprisoned for it.

The story kept going on for pages and pages, and I kept reading, wanting to find out what would happen to this poor guy Joseph. Lo and behold, it turned out he could interpret dreams because he was touched by God.

Word of this remarkable Joseph reached the Egyptian pharaoh, who was troubled by his own dreams and beckoned the lowly prisoner to interpret them. After assuring Pharaoh only God knows what his dreams mean, Joseph relayed to the Egyptian ruler what the dreams portended, that there would be years of feast, followed by famine, throughout the land.

The ruler, so moved by Joseph's abilities, put him in charge of Egypt, and the former prisoner ordered the people to conserve food while it was plentiful to save for the day when the famine would come. And it came. So all Joseph did was save the lives of millions.

I think my sister Kathy knew the story already. But sitting across from me at the dining room table late that night in New York City, she humored me. Because I was trying to make a point. That maybe, there was a reason for suffering, even if we couldn't see it in the moment, even if we didn't understand it. That good could come from the anguish, from the inexplicable.

A day later, my father was less amused by the inexplicable—especially the inexplicable rumor he'd heard from other family members: That I'd drawn close to the teachings of Jesus. What's this all about? There was a discernible expression of consternation on his face. It was a gaunt look. Hollowed out cheeks. He survived his suicide attempt, but the remnants still showed, a kind of frailty from the trauma.

No longer hospitalized, he was convalescing in a rehab center. It was a converted old grand house, plantation style, at the top of a rise on the outskirts of New York. Big rooms, filled with nooks and crannies.

My father had a roommate, a twenty-something-year-old named Peter. A good guy. Actually, everyone but my father in the house was in their twenties, and most of them were festooned with tattoos. All suffered from substance addictions. Alcohol. Illicit drugs. Prescription medication. My father reported, his housemates called each other "dude" and "bro." Sometimes, they went surfing. Not his thing. He'd stay behind and puff on a cigar.

The way he explained it, my father didn't try to kill himself because of me. Or I wasn't the only culprit, as I saw it. He insisted my ruination wasn't the cause of his. He had his own problems, unbeknownst to the rest of the family, least of all to me.

He and I had grown distant over the years, hardly talked, barely ever saw each other. I'd never forgiven him for what he did to my mother, all those years ago, leaving her without a penny, forcing her into destitution, while he kidnapped my sister and me when we were children, keeping us in hiding as he sent us to a therapist who brainwashed us into believing our mother was unfit, turning us against our mother, using the man's molestation of me against her, leaving our mother childless. (Five-second version of a defining experience.)

As an adult, I had told my father I blamed him for what he did, indicting him for past sins. So we lived our separate lives, my father and me. But strangely enough, my father and I found ourselves in similar situations now.

We had almost nothing but despair. He tried to kill himself just as I was consumed with thoughts of ending it all. His life, as he knew it, was over. My life, as I knew it, was over. My ruination was worse than his, of course, but nobody said this was a competition, right?

It was left to each of us to decide what to do with the blown-up pieces. Our own experiences of destruction occurred almost simultaneously. The synchronized detonation in time was curious. What were we to make of it? I didn't know yet.

We sat stiffly at a diner near the rehab center, squeezed around a table with my older sister Karen and her precocious daughter. That's when my father brought up Jesus. What's going on with *that*?

I was a bit caught off guard. We'd been chitchatting

about nothing in particular over a club sandwich and pancakes. We hadn't been talking about faith. It was a non sequitur. I asked him whether he'd read the Gospels? No. He told me he once thought about writing a book about Jesus. That surprised me. Well, why don't you read the Gospels? Or how about reading that book I sent, *The Case for Christ*? My father promised he would. I wasn't so sure.

At that point, the only thing I was sure of was this: What was happening to me felt almost biblical, the loss of nearly everything: My career, my reputation, everything I built over decades. I also knew I was about to lose my job, my income. I didn't know how I was going to support my family, my children. I was on the verge of signing over the house to Julie-Ann, effectively making me homeless. I lost friends, I lost colleagues, I lost therapists, I lost lawyers, I lost my literary agent, I lost my book deal, I lost my Fulbright. Heck, my bank account was about to be looted by someone who would steal my identity. Yes, really. I was about to become the victim of identity theft. Someone was about to take my *identity*. Obviously, whoever absconded with my identity hadn't bothered to read my press clippings or they would have taken a pass and stolen someone else less besmirched.

But what next? Frogs? Hail? Locust?

When I finally heard from the university investigator, it came, as I knew it would, in an email.

Months earlier, the university showed its hand when a top school official told one of my attorneys the university would have to go through with its investigation of me or face the ire of the organized group publicly attacking me. That left the university only one choice in how to deal with me.

It still hit me like a wrecking ball. The university investigator decided, in her opinion, I violated university policies involving five people, including the former employee I let go, even though she never accused me of misconduct when she was a graduate student of mine nearly a decade earlier, or when she worked for me about five years earlier.

The university investigator's opinion was so shocking—as was the basis for it: She believed unverified innuendo and unsubstantiated words of accusers, who had a clear agenda, even though there was no proof I did anything wrong.

Equally shocking, the university investigator decided to believe I violated university policies involving the three former students from several years ago who also had an ax to grind but until now had never accused me of anything. These three leveled the worst of the allegations—of touching: a shirt tag, patting a shoulder to say it's going to be okay, standing back to back to compare heights.

And the fifth and final: The university investigator somehow, inexplicably, decided I violated university policies involving a student from many years ago who was never a student of mine, over whom I had no authority, a former student who, in her own words, said I was a nice person, she often misinterpreted people, and she wasn't sure I did anything except be kind to her. That was the upshot of alleged diary excerpts the university investigator let me glance at for a few moments. The university investigator decided I spoke inappropriately with this former student, including complimenting her, in crowded public settings—a school cafeteria and a school dinner function.

In her conclusions, the university investigator didn't say I propositioned any students. She didn't say I intentionally laid a finger on anyone. No one accused me of anything of the sort, despite the wildly false stories in the media. Indeed, for most of the complaints of alleged misconduct, the investigator could not bring herself to reach the conclusion I did anything wrong, but she said that was to be expected. Wait. What?

I'm not sure why that was to be expected. As a veteran investigative journalist, I knew it would have been *unexpected* that most of the allegations fell through, how they didn't amount to anything, unless there was a problem with the whole set of allegations. That so many accusations amounted to nothing, even to a university investigator who seemed bent on believing them, should have suggested a major red flag, especially since most referenced conversations occurred at least five years earlier, many nearly a decade ago.

As shocking as it was, I'd already concluded there wasn't anything fair about this process; the university investigator had the power to effectively rule however she wanted, and she worked for the university, which, it seemed obvious, needed to protect its self-interest. To protect its reputation against the maelstrom of bad publicity in the news being generated by the organized campaign of attackers. I was collateral damage.

It didn't matter that I produced more than seven *hundred* pages of documents for the university contradicting virtually every allegation, including scores of emails from the former students who, now, years later, were accusing me of mistreatment.

Had I produced *seven* emails, not scores, that would have been a lot, given that most of what was alleged occurred many years ago in conversations.

It didn't matter I was never accused of mistreating any students in all of my decade at Northwestern in any of the anonymous student evaluations the university officially used to help assess professors.

Disregarding those hundreds of pages of documents, my professorial colleague, working with the university investigator, decided to conclude in favor of almost every instance when a student accused me of being tough, or unfair.

Never mind if any professor is anything of the kind to students, it is inconceivable for that behavior not to be called out in the anonymous student evaluations. It is inconceivable that a student wouldn't ever complain to a university official—any university official—about any misconduct over a decade if there was any misconduct. But they didn't. Because it never happened. Indeed, it is simply impossible, over a decade, for students to not ever accuse you anonymously of any misconduct if it happened.

What mattered was what I was going to do at this point. And the options weren't good. I could keep fighting, which was another way of saying I could continue to drain the family assets, because, according to one leading attorney in this field, it would cost an additional $50,000, give or take, in legal fees to continue to engage in the university process.

Then I took a look at the fine print. Not good either. From what I could gather, I could appeal the university investigator's conclusion to a dizzying array of other university people, bodies, and hearings, but the basis on which I could appeal was so narrowly defined, it made it virtually impossible to challenge whatever the university investigator decided.

I couldn't help but come to the understanding that the university investigator's opinion, in effect, wasn't designed to be challenged. Had I any doubts about that, the university dispelled them quickly.

The university promptly issued a public statement to the media, applauding the bravery of those who came forward to file complaints against me and apologizing for their suffering. And yet, there was no final determination, I wasn't given the opportunity to appeal yet, I hadn't even decided if I was going to appeal, the process was still ongoing.

Throughout the months, even as the university put out its public statement, the school continued to admonish me to keep silent because this was supposed to be a confidential process. So much for the idea of due process, a fair hearing.

This reminded me of the flaws in the U.S. criminal

justice system. I spent years examining murder cases, investigating wrongful convictions, and here's what became all too evident: When you're convicted of a crime, it's incredibly difficult to overturn that conviction, no matter how insane the process, no matter how unfair.

Now, here I was. Not accused of a crime. But ensnared in a process that dawned on me offered no real promise of an appeal. Forget the cost of continuing to try to defend myself. Leave aside the pummeling I was taking in the media. The toll on my family was so severe, it was hard to fathom, when my daughter, at random moments, would ask me if I was still employed, whether the investigation was over. Julie-Ann was suffering immensely; her mother, a great woman of faith, received a bad diagnosis in the midst of my ordeal. It was just too much for Julie-Ann, the constant and intense bulldozing darkness so stifling, she would turn off the lights before dark and go to sleep almost from the moment she came home from work as an elementary school aide.

Now I had a deeper appreciation for why plea deals are one of the leading forms of wrongful convictions. Sometimes people don't fight to the end—don't *want* to fight to the end—even when they're innocent, because they recognize the process is stacked against them, that no matter how much evidence they produce proving their innocence, they are going down. The emotional toll is too overwhelming. The cost is so mammoth. The risk of an uncertain future is too great: Gamble you might get the death penalty or make a deal for your life without parole? I'd heard the stories, talked to inmates. They'd cop a plea. They'd agree to settle the case. They just wanted to end the agony.

I wanted it to end, too. I didn't care about what it meant for me. My life was over. I just wanted the suffering to end for my children, for my family. They'd endured more than enough for months.

My mother left a tearful voicemail, telling me to resign from the university, to forget about the appeals process, to just let it all go. My older sister Karen had some choice words for the university, for those who publicly attacked me. Karen was always the tough one in the family.

My younger sister Kathy talked me through the various scenarios, and we kept running into the same wall of inevitability, the appeals process was pointless. My father reached the same conclusion as did Julie-Ann. Had I any doubts, they were removed when I spoke to a couple of lawyers who were helping me for free as friends after I got rid of a bunch of other attorneys who weren't free.

As a favor, one of the lawyer acquaintances was communicating with the university on my behalf when suddenly and inexplicably she refused to speak to me unless it was in the presence of another attorney acquaintance, who sent me a strongly worded email to that effect. Not terribly friendly. It was the oddest thing, as if the one attorney acquaintance was representing the other, not me. I had no idea why. It couldn't be good. But I had no fight left. I just wanted it to be over. Finally, I decided to put an end to all of it.

In the end, I wasn't sanctioned in any way. I wasn't fired. I didn't go through the university appeals process. There was no final determination. I walked away.

I figured someone would leak the news of my departure, which was only supposed to be known to the university and me. I figured right. On the day I stepped down, I began hearing from news outlets. The university permitted me to issue my own public statement, approving the specific language. I wanted it to be clear I voluntarily resigned. This was my choice. While writing the statement, I added I believed this was "in the best interests of everyone involved." Julie-Ann, reviewing my draft, wanted to know why I wanted to add that part. Because I believed it. I prayed to God about what to say, and I believed this was in fact in everyone's best interests.

It was in the best interests of my children, who wouldn't have to read more news articles about their father, presented as the monster. It was in the best interests of Julie-Ann, who I worried couldn't take the emotional and physical toll any more. It was in the best interests of the university to get rid of me to avoid further negative publicity from my attackers.

It was also in the best interests of the accusers to see me gone, to see me give up my career, to resign as a full, tenured professor, to see my public fall from grace end in a resounding crash. They wanted blood, and that's what they got in great measure.

Some of the attackers, no doubt, were swept up in the

fervor of the moment, but some of them must have felt it was deserved, that they had been wronged, or why else would they want to destroy so utterly? When I prayed, I asked for their forgiveness. I prayed, hoping they would one day forgive me for whatever they felt—anger, hurt, disappointment. I prayed they would forgive me for the flawed person I am, for not doing better, for not understanding enough, for all my many imperfections. When I prayed, I also forgave them. I felt no anger. I wished only goodness for those who attacked me, who destroyed me.

There was a silver lining of sorts. With my resignation, I didn't have to submit a Faculty Activity Report. I was spared that annual chore, answering a bunch of questions in tons of pages I always wondered if anyone ever bothered to read. That mystery would have to remain unsolved. I was done with that epic task. Okay. Fine. Not much of a silver lining.

chapter ten

I'm lost; there are too many moving parts, I need to walk Rosie, feed her, get the kids up, but my son doesn't know how the knobs on the shower work, so we get sogging wet, and I have to ride herd, telling my daughter to get hustling because she's sleepy and not getting ready, and, oh my goodness, we're running late, we're not going to get to each of their schools on time—come to think of it, I'm not even sure how to get to either place—and, oh, wait, I have to make breakfast, but there's nothing in the fridge other than day-old pizza, a cardboard-like turd if I've ever seen one, which will have to do, after I zap it for thirty seconds in the microwave, and then we're off, out the door, I'm still in my pajamas and slippers, and Rosie's hopping in the front seat of the old clunker because she wants to be in on the action, tail wagging, except then a question forms as I peer over my shoulder at the kids in the back seat: Did you brush your teeth?

Silence fills the air. Ugh.

Then it gets worse. I'm pulling up to my daughter's school, but apparently I'm also breaking every unspoken rule of the dreaded car line. I'm unintentionally choking traffic on the narrow street in front of her school to the point no other car can pass. Parents are honking. I can see their faces fuming, arms gesticulating, and mouths moving behind the glass of their car windows. Good thing I can't hear their vitriol. I smile and shrug, as if to say: I'm new, I'm sorry, I didn't get the dreaded car line manual, I don't know how this works. The pantomime doesn't work. I'm afraid I'm going to be arrested by the car line police.

Somehow, my daughter quickly slips out of the car and into the school building, and I escape, until the next crucible: my son's car line.

By the time we get there, we're already way back, so far behind the other cars snaking in line, we're more than a block away, out of view of the school, practically in another state. When we finally arrive at the front of the line, I'm exhausted, drained, defeated, ready for a nap. I tell my son

I love him. He mumbles the same and slams the door.

This is going to be harder than I thought.

Okay. Let me explain, just in case it isn't obvious: I'm unemployed. Check that. I'm *unemployable.* Julie-Ann, by contrast, is perfectly employable. That's why she quit her job. We couldn't afford it. You don't want to know what a school aide makes.

Now, she's in sales. No pressure, though. Her salary is based on commission. I haven't left the house and found my own place to live. Someone has to look after the kids while she goes to work. She'd done it for years as a stay-at-home mom. Now it's my turn.

Anyway, the point is, from the get-go, Julie-Ann is up and out the door, and she's usually not back until the evening. That leaves me as—let me see—how about this? Executive Director of Household Management.

I'm the maid. I make the beds. I wash the dishes. I do the laundry. It's a new gig for me. After years of shaving and showering before heading into an office, pajamas are absolutely acceptable attire. Slippers will do just fine. A hat can cover my unkempt hair, but—let's be real—the hat is optional.

This should be a piece of cake, right? Wrong. The grocery store is a mysterious house of mirrors that leaves me in a puddle of confusion. I need a tour guide and a map of the layout of this epic place, particularly when I'm asked to fetch a specific obscure item, like baking soda, which, for the life of me, makes no sense either. What do you do with baking soda? It's not like you can just eat baking soda, or can you? Imagine me racing down aisles, as if enduring an obstacle course, but with no finish line.

And just when I made the beds, it seems they need to be made again. Same with the dishes. I just washed them, and there they are again, needing another washing. Ditto the laundry. It never ends. It just piles up again. There's no sense of completion. Sense of treadmill, maybe.

Maybe I should've seen it coming. Not just the treadmill. The fall, too. In the days before the destruction, when I had no idea how my life was about to blow up, in the peaceful interlude, I was in southern California with my students, investigating a quadruple homicide.

We'd driven into horse country, made our way up a winding hill, and parked in search of a crime scene. There was some question about which house was which. The murders occurred nearly forty years earlier. The homes weren't clearly marked. Maybe they'd changed postal numbers. Maybe they didn't exist anymore. What remained were the horrific crime scene photos, which I reviewed in a cold storage facility under the steady gaze of a retired FBI agent who investigated the case at no cost for the prisoner and firmly believed in the innocence of the accused who sat on death row, awaiting his execution.

For all the murders I investigated, I never saw such frenzied savagery. I never saw photos of this level of unadulterated, depraved evil before. Two small children were hacked to death. There was evidence one child, the little girl, almost escaped before being dragged back into the house in her nightgown. The parents of the little girl were attacked with what appeared to be an ax and large blade while they slept.

It appeared the killer—or killers—arranged the bodies after the mayhem. The father was left in a kneeling prayer position. The mother's body was laid out, cross-like. There appeared to be a series of small surface puncture wounds—post mortem—on the little girl, as if they were left there like some kind of satanic ritual.

Authorities concluded this was a robbery gone bad. But that didn't make sense to me. All manner of valuables, including a wad of cash, remained in plain view. The car keys were left in the unlocked cars. And why kill the children? Why the butchery? Why? Why? *Why?* I couldn't really comprehend what I was looking at. I couldn't get it out of my mind. Still can't. I wouldn't want that kind of memory branding for my students. There was no need. The crimes were memorialized in the police records, in the court documents. The students didn't need to view this kind of bloody nightmare.

What they saw instead was a nondescript man standing outside a little shack of a house on the side of the hill. We approached him. He was friendly. Turned out, he lived there. Somehow, he got on the topic of telling us his life story. How he lost his tech job. How it was hard to reinvent himself at his age. I distinctly remember thinking, he's about *my* age. What would I do? I shuddered at the thought. I wasn't qualified to do much of anything. He was handy, though, so he became a handyman, fixing things. I distinctly remember thinking, I'm *not* handy. I can't fix things. So he settled into this shack behind him, fixing things.

Well, anyway, he got around to pointing up the hill at the house, the site of the murders, and waved us on our way. I distinctly remember feeling a vague uncomfortableness about the encounter. Not only about the murders. But about his story, the end of life as he knew it.

This was just days before the end of my life as I knew it, just before the public attacks. I didn't give it much credence, the meaning of the encounter. But was it a sign of my impending loss? I'd been recently drawn to other stories of a similar design. I watched a movie on my iPhone about a chef who finds himself ridiculed on the internet, loses his job, and seeks to find himself. Starting all over, going back to basics, he makes Cuban sandwiches on a food truck and, in the process, draws closer to his family. Then I watched the movie again, pleasant noise in the background while I did something else, like vacuuming. When my son wanted to watch it, I saw it yet again. I'm not sure why. It just resonated, aside from my predilection for Cuban sandwiches.

Was I being acclimated to what was about to happen, to my own unemployment, my own public ridicule? Was this pointing the way forward? Or was it just the way I was, instinctively drawn to stories of redemption, of a Hollywood mirage?

The subtleties escaped me. But I begin to pick up on these: I already planned tomorrow's breakfast. I shopped for the apple danish my son likes, the fresh baked bread my daughter prefers. I knew where to locate them in the supermarket—haha! I set my alarm hours before I needed to wake the kids. I knew I would probably wake up without any prompting before daylight anyway. Couldn't be helped. But just in case.

By the time I woke the kids, I'd already lived a lifetime. I walked Rosie, diced her organic chicken and jasmine rice. I made my four shots of espresso. I sat at my laptop writing this—whatever you want to call it—my story, my testimony. I taught my son how to turn the knobs of the shower. Nobody got sprayed anymore. I double-checked to make sure my daughter was awake and stirring. I kept them on the clock, on schedule. I bark out a variation of a phrase from a Stephen King prison movie they've never seen: Dufresne, you're holding up the line! They had no idea who Dufresne was. Didn't matter. They got the idea. By the time they piled downstairs, breakfast was already on the table.

There was a rhythm to the routine with the kids. When I made their school snack and lunch, I drew little pictures of Rosie on the paper bags, along with a little note, that I loved them. The kids remembered to brush their teeth. Rosie hopped in the front seat of the car. We took a shortcut to my daughter's school. We were way ahead of the dreaded car line. I waved to Katie, a mother in the neighborhood. She waved back. I exchanged recipes with other mothers. I coined a phrase I repeated every morning to my daughter as she climbed out of the car: "Be bold, be brave, be careful, have a great day, and I love you." Off she went.

My son was next. We were at the front of his car line. No more waiting for this muchacho. I nodded to the crossing guard. He nodded back. We were buds now. I offered up the same mantra to my son: "Be bold, be brave, be careful, have a great day, and I love you."

When I picked up the kids after school, I heard their rambling stories and scandals du jour. So-and-so wasn't friends with such-and-such anymore. Missus something-or-other was a great teacher. My daughter wanted to try out for the school musical. Go for it. My son wanted to sign up for Mathnasium. *What?* He was volunteering for an after-school program to learn more math. He was already great at it. He wanted to be better, to hone his greatness. My goodness. I peered at him in the rearview mirror. *What?* That was the look on his inscrutable cherub of a nine-year-old face. Couldn't argue with that.

I thought of his looming homework. We'd be at the kitchen table soon trying to work it out together. It occurred to me fourth-grade math wasn't what it used to be. I could knock that out of the park, once of yore. Now, not so much. True, I can barely remember division. I have to double-check my subtraction. But. Still. What was with all the complicated equations and diagrams? When did nine-year-olds need to know all these hieroglyphics? Mathnasium was suddenly looking pretty darn good. Sure, I tell my son. We'll sign you up.

It's not like I didn't know what was going on before. It's just that before, I traveled a good bit, visiting prisons tucked away from civilization, meeting convicted killers, investigating wrongful convictions throughout the United States. Sometimes, I'd get home late. Sometimes, I'd miss important moments, like the first time my daughter mastered her bicycle, after we practiced for days. I always brought home gifts from my travels, but it didn't matter. It didn't make up for my absence. The kids dreaded my next trip. Rosie too. She'd have trouble pooping. Sorry. TMI.

Now, though, I *really* knew what was going on. Like they wanted french fries and cheeseburgers and ice cream from McDonald's after I picked them up from school. I looked around. There was no higher authority than me in the car. We sped off to the drive-through to stuff our faces with junk food.

Some things never change. Even before the destruction, before it all went away, I was the pushover, or the security blanket, depending on the point of view. I'd put my children down to sleep if I got home in time. It was a night-time process that, for years, would take hours, after I told them stories—and they better be good—none of this trite pitter-patter of once upon a time.

They wanted real drama, unexpected plot twists, and a rousing denouement. For my daughter, we reached triple digits in chapters of one storyline, "The Princess of the Rainbow," a tale of a little girl who overcomes witches and other terrors of the night.

In the evenings, I read books to my children, including the *Harry Potter* series, especially when I realized my son was not only paying attention, but was riveted to the plot, so much so he was developing theories about Snape, one of the main characters. At night, I sang songs to my children, which constituted my full repertoire of the National Anthem and the Beatles and not much else.

Now, though, the night-time routine reflected a new stage: I made a candle-lit dinner for the kids, with mood music: The Eagles wafting in the background, accompanying my masterpiece of fried chicken, or pasta—not spaghetti—with garlic and pancetta—not ham.

Then we retired to the living room where my daughter would intently draw, paint, and create arts and crafts, while my son saddled into his Xbox, ensconced in his headset, jabbering with his friends online. Later, Julie-Ann would be upstairs asleep, exhausted after another long day in the trenches. Rosie would be curled up next to me on the floor while I read another book about Jesus. When it was time, we prayed and headed upstairs for the night.

The kids were growing up.

Not so long ago, it seemed, my daughter used a pink binkie, which I've stored for years in my dresser drawer, back behind the socks for safekeeping. Not so long ago, my son used to play with his Legos. Well, he used to play with some of his Legos while, in his self-anointed role as Social Director of the Living Room, assigning me to build ornate castles from thick Lego instruction booklets that would take me about four hours in the middle of the night before he wrecked them in the morning, *kapow*.

Now the pieces sit untouched in a bin.

I guess this is a strange way of being a little thankful for the destruction, for the losses. Had it not been for what happened, I wouldn't be here. I wouldn't have these beautiful moments with the kids—moments I'll never get back—heading upstairs after spending another quiet evening being closely connected in time and place.

I'm not saying I'd want to go through the agony again— just in case *anyone* is listening. But. Still. When I prayed to God, I was thankful. I accepted where I was, what was to come. I recognized, in my misfortune, I was kind of fortunate.

It wasn't just being with the kids. I was able to help dozens of women gain their freedom in Oklahoma. That, in turn, touched their children, their families, their communities. There was even hope for Amber, who was sentenced to life in prison after failing drug court. She passed the first stage of her commutation request, winning the unanimous approval of the parole board to move to the second stage: A personal appearance to tell her story and possibly convince the board to recommend her freedom to the governor.

I'm not sure how many other inmates would have won their freedom had it not been for my own misfortune. Sorry about the double negative. The point is, I'd have missed out on all those opportunities to help others. I'd have been entrenched in my old life, perhaps too comfortable, perhaps sticking with it too long.

I always told my students they couldn't succeed without being willing to fail. I always said: What is the point of tackling an investigation unless it's difficult? Who else was going to do it—to investigate a wrongful conviction—if we didn't? Where was the fun in it if it was too easy? You don't play the angles. You don't look for the quick victory. You don't achieve greatness by playing it safe. I always believed in my own competency.

Now, though, I was going to have to live up to my own blustery words. If I was going to keep going, I would need to rebuild from less than zero. This wasn't going to be easy. I didn't really have any other choice, though. Not if I wanted to be there for my children, for my family, for Rosie. I would have to embrace the challenge.

chapter eleven

Death at seventy miles an hour is a funny thing. Okay. Not
funny. But strange. Or so I surmise as I briefly lose control
of the wheel of the car after the passenger-side tire blows
out on the highway.

I'm not worried in the slightest. I placidly see it all happening in slow motion. Rumble of the stripped wheel, metal
grinding against concrete. Smoke rises from the blowout.
The car veers slightly off the road into a bank of threadbare
brush and grass.

This might be it. I'm okay with that. I'm at peace with

the conclusive, concussive idea. I can see what is about to happen in my mind's eye, the car flipping over, glass shattering, metal crushing me to death.

But then—in the ensuing seconds—something takes hold of me. Sanity? Insanity? God? All I know is, I realize I'm not driving my own car. This is *Kevin's* car. My old friend. He lent me his car. I can't total it. Suddenly, I take a firmer grip of the wheel, press on the brake, wresting back control of the wayward vehicle, steering it to a quiet stop on the shoulder of the highway.

Maybe another day.

A moment later, a state trooper pulls over. What happened? Not sure. He tells me tires blow out all the time on this stretch of highway between Oklahoma City and Tulsa. No accounting for it. I had just left Mabel Bassett, a prison for women on a road called Kickapoo, when the car inconvenienced me with possible death.

The state trooper drives off, leaving me standing in the grass, waiting for AAA to show up and replace the tire, feeling the whoosh of eighteen-wheelers barreling by. And I'm thinking, maybe I should have been afraid. Maybe I shouldn't have welcomed it so much. Maybe not everything has been resolved. It's not exactly the optimal state of mind I'm needing on the eve of returning to class. Yes. I'm returning to class—not as a professor but as a student. First time in, oh, a million years or so.

I'm about to take a required class for an Oklahoma

license to become a private investigator. Here's my thinking: I'm already investigating cases in Oklahoma, working with the nonprofit, Another Chance Justice Project, to help incarcerated women.

Plus, there's this minor issue: I need a job. I'm not sure how I'm going to support my family. My career in academia is over. What's more, given my public ruination, I figure nobody would risk hiring me to work in an office—any office—which covers a rather wide spectrum of professions, including my old one, as an investigative journalist. That position usually involves an office, a newsroom, at one point or another.

But who said I can't be my own boss? Why can't I consider hiring myself to work for me as a private investigator? I might even give myself a job. I don't know much, but I know how to find stuff out, especially hard-to-find stuff. The real question now is, do I still remember how to take proper notes in class? Even more, do I still have the attention span to sit in a classroom from 9:00 A.M. to 4:30 P.M. for a full week? Because that's what I just signed up for.

The answer, I quickly surmise, is an unequivocal no.

That's my conclusion on the first day in a small strip mall in a small office building in a small classroom, featuring a large plastic garbage bin to catch water dripping from the ceiling.

The instructor is discussing Eisenhower. As in Dwight D. The former president. From the 1950s. We're in the *1950s*. What does this have to do with learning to become a licensed private investigator? Absolutely nothing.

My eyes are darting around, trying to see if my class-mates are awe-struck by this monumental digression, but all I gather are attentive faces intently listening to the instructor who proceeds to go through the rest of the presidents of the United States after Eisenhower with assorted trivia. In reverse chronology: Kennedy, Johnson, Nixon—let's not forget Ford—Carter, Reagan, Bush One, Clinton, Bush Two, Obama, and Trump. Not a single one is left out. Political opinion and theory are shared galore.

I'd be worried, except my eyes are drooping, and I'm straining not to fall asleep in a hard metal chair. Maybe I do pass out. Because the next thing I know, the instructor is talking about private investigator material that will be on the state exam. But wait. He stops. He apologizes. He tells us he recently had a stroke. He can't remember sometimes. He has notes. But he can't remember where he put them. I'm worried about him. No need. He gets on a roll. He's talking about state law, digital cameras, secret recording devices. He knows what he's talking about. I'm beginning to feel like I do too. I ace the daily quizzes. My memory is intact. I can still read a textbook chapter and instantly remember pertinent details.

But before I pat myself on the back for still being a nerd, I'm also beginning to feel uneasy. I'm not comfortable with some of the lessons. Not the information, per se. But the ethics behind them.

It's stated, without an iota of concern, you can pretend to be someone you're not to gather information as a private investigator. You can, for instance, pose as an employee of a company to gain the trust of other workers as a way of finding out what's really going on. This is called "pretext." I call it deception. It's not allowed in investigative journalism, at least not the kind I practiced for years. If you lie about who you are, then how do we know you're not lying about something else, including the information you obtained?

The class textbook, without batting an eyelash, also talks about how private investigators use surveillance. Maybe this should have been obvious to me. I mean, who hasn't seen a movie where a private eye secretly records someone? But now that I'm learning about it, it's sinking in. And I don't like the idea of sneaking around. It isn't what I've done as an investigative reporter. It's not what I've taught my students of investigative journalism. Always be honest. Be honorable. There are no shortcuts.

Which brings me to another technique of the private investigator I can't stomach. They can pay sources for information. It's presented as no big deal. But it is to me. Because I've never done it as an investigative reporter. Because how do you know your source is telling the truth when you pay them for information? What if they're telling you whatever they're telling you simply for the money? How reliable is that information?

Cheryl, a classmate, asks if I want to grab lunch. She

mentions she noticed how I came to class, crossing a busy intersection, dodging traffic, on foot. No car. I'm unshaven. She insists on paying for my gyro sandwich. She's taking mercy on me. The hobo. I fit the profile. I look like I should be on a street corner with an empty cup.

I don't yet have the opportunity to explain that I'm from out of town, another state, staying at a nearby extended-stay hotel, while taking this class. Instead, we commiserate over gyros. She's stunned as much as I am about the instruction, particularly the part about the presidents of the United States. All this time, I thought I was the only one. I make a mental note about my classmates: Learn to read poker faces better.

I'm even more stunned by another fact. Cheryl tells me why she's here. She's a hairdresser. But she served as a juror in a heinous murder trial. And she couldn't believe what she witnessed, the tremendous fallibility of the system, the way it *doesn't* work, how someone can be accused and found guilty of a crime, even when the facts clearly point in another direction.

Cheryl tells me it's bothered her so much, stayed with her so deeply, it compelled her to be here. To take this class. To take the state exam. To become a licensed private investigator. I haven't said much of anything, partly because I'm enjoying the gyro sandwich, partly because Cheryl is so passionate about what she's saying the words are just tumbling out. I wait for a small opening.

Then I tell her. What I've done over the past several

years is investigate wrongful convictions. Now I have her attention. What I'm doing now is helping excessively sentenced women fight for their freedom through parole or commutation.

I'm not sure Cheryl believes me. I mean, what are the chances? That this is what means so much to her and that this is what I'm doing? This was just supposed to be lunch over gyros. I can tell, though, Cheryl's going to be a great private investigator. Me? I'm not so sure.

By week's end, as the class comes to a close, I'm nearly ready to take the state exam. I'm pretty darn sure I'd pass if I took it right then. But I'm also pretty sure I'm not going to do this. Not just not take the state exam. But *not* become a private investigator. It's not me. This isn't what I do.

I spent a small fortune on the requisite class, on the license application, on the required bond insurance, on the creation of an Oklahoma limited liability company, on an unpublished website I spent hours noodling over. I also obtained fingerprints, got background checked in three different municipalities, and took a bad passport photo.

Now I undid it all. I withdrew from the second required class. I withdrew my license application. I canceled the bond insurance. I dissolved my Oklahoma LLC. I resigned as a Department of Corrections volunteer. All I had to show for my efforts: A certificate of completion for my private investigator course. I ruefully thought of the certificate of completion I made for inmates. My fancy piece of paper was worth a lot less than theirs.

I'd been sensing things were coming to an end in Oklahoma. It wasn't just the class. There were other signs. One was forty-six pounds. As in forty-six pounds of marijuana. Let me explain.

Things got to the point at Another Chance Justice Project where the system was working. Virtually every prisoner we sought to help with their parole gained their freedom. Trish and Kate, two of my nonprofit colleagues, mastered the process. Indeed, they surpassed me.

In reviewing cases, Trish came across Vanessa, an inmate who was caught trying to transport forty-six pounds of marijuana. That, by the way, is a lot of weed.

Had I been reviewing Vanessa's case, I'm not sure I would have picked her as a candidate for our support. I mean, it's not like she was caught with a little roach of marijuana in the vehicle's cigarette ashtray. We were talking *forty-six* pounds. That took room. That required logistics and transportation.

But Trish checked it out, and she was convinced Vanessa deserved a second chance at freedom. Trish asked me to speak with Vanessa. Not only that, but Trish figured out a way to call the prison to get Vanessa on the phone. That in itself was impressive. Typically, you couldn't just call over to a prison and ask to speak to an inmate. You had to jump through a bunch of bureaucratic hoops, register your credit card through a complicated automated system from the netherworld, and then wait for the inmate to call you. Not Trish, though. She just called and—voila—I was speaking with Vanessa. I asked about her case, about her background, about her life before prison, as a maid who barely survived, who made no excuses for the forty-six pounds.

Vanessa made a mistake, a big mistake, and she paid dearly for it in prison. I got off the call. Trish was right. We ought to help Vanessa even if parole looked like a long shot. With Kate's help, I immediately drafted a letter of support from the nonprofit to the parole board. I figured there was no chance, nil, except, as it happened, there was.

Vanessa ended up winning her freedom. When it happened, I thought of the sense of lightness she must have felt, that it was over, the prison punishment. I couldn't call her, so I did the next best thing. I called Trish and congratulated her. Various expletives flowed from her. Had it not been for Trish, Vanessa might not have made it out. I told Trish she didn't need me anymore, that the nonprofit didn't need me anymore. My work was done. I was kidding. But I suppose sometimes there's a kernel of truth in a joke.

It was, after all, time for me to step aside. I loved my colleagues at the nonprofit. I would miss them dearly. But I'd been ignoring the inevitable. I had a family to feed. I needed to figure out how to make a living. And fast. A full-time job would be helpful to avoid becoming homeless. I let go of Oklahoma.

The hardest part was letting go of the inmates I was

helping. They called all the time. Now, I needed to let them know someone else would be helping them. Someone else from the nonprofit, Another Chance Justice Project. I worried for them. I spoke with their mothers and daughters. I pored over the details of their cases. Okay. Fine. Perhaps I was a bit obsessive compulsive.

I always viewed myself as just an insignificant cog in a great big machine, a replaceable widget in the grand scheme of life. Besides, I had faith in my colleagues at Another Chance Justice Project. They could ably handle everything. The inmates would be just fine without me. That's what I told Amber when she called. But she was serving a life sentence after failing drug court, and not everything was fine.

Amber told me she relied on our weekly calls when we reviewed her case. We went over details of her upcoming commutation hearing, seeking her freedom. She read aloud the prepared remarks she planned to give to the parole board. I gave her my two cents. Amber didn't want me to go. She told me, "You're my person."

Well. When you put it like that. I called Trish at Another Chance Justice Project. We agreed, I'd keep helping Amber. It wasn't just that I was her person. It wasn't just that I'd been investigating her case for more than a year—long before I got to Oklahoma, back in my former life, when I ran The Medill Justice Project, when I first heard about her plight. Amber's situation was different because her case was live—it was in the midst of being considered by the parole board. Her personal appearance—a crucial moment that could be the difference between freedom and prison—was scheduled for December, just weeks away.

She still faced long odds. But this wasn't the time to go away. This was the time to see it through. I let Amber know. I was with her until the end, whatever the outcome might be. Amber let me know she was relieved, though I didn't deserve that. We resumed our weekly calls like nothing changed. Except I was back in Illinois. And I was staring at my computer screen.

Now what?

Even more to the point: What was I qualified to do to make a living?

This was about the time I wished I were a farmer. Now, that was a solid line of work, cultivating the soil. Or wouldn't it have been nice if I had another *real* skill, like plumbing or electrical work? People always need a plumber or an electrician. Heck, I would have been happy to know how to cook with any real semblance of competence. Except I was a danger in the kitchen, aside from being a rank amateur of fine cuisine. Once, while trying to separate frozen hamburger patties, the dinner knife slipped and stabbed me in the hand. Blood gushed everywhere. I ended up in the ER getting stitched up. I was a bystander to this episode. Okay. Not really. I stabbed myself, strictly speaking. But the point was, I couldn't think of anything I could do, any non-dangerous tradable skill I possessed.

Except how to write. But what was I going to do with that?

I looked online. It was bleak. Job descriptions yawned before me, remote contract technical writing positions that called for a working knowledge of search engine optimization, otherwise known as SEO, and other acronyms that made absolutely no intelligible sense to me. Editing jobs were there for the taking if you knew about work management flow systems or some such gobbledygook in arcane fields involving factories about which I knew nada.

So I applied to them. All of them. Every day. Tons of them. I had no idea what they were, these writing gigs in faraway places and distant lands. They didn't require my physical presence. I could work from my laptop at Starbucks, for all they cared. But they paid. Not much. The calculus, however, was pretty simple. Money was going out of the house. None was coming in.

It got to the point I almost felt like I reached the end of the internet. There were no more jobs to which I could apply. I'd seen them all. I'd exhausted all the possibilities. And I got a positive response from exactly—zippo. I did receive a few automated emails—stragglers—that thanked me for applying and informing me I wasn't what they were seeking because who needs a bestselling author and an award-winning journalist formerly of the *Washington Post* and *Wall Street Journal* to do their technical writing about knobs and widgets? Okay. Fine. They didn't mention the last part.

What was left unstated was the digital world had passed me by. Writing, to a large extent, wasn't about writing anymore. It was largely about social media. Maximizing eyeballs. Using short bursts of words without punctuation—140 characters, including blank spaces—to raise visibility, to enhance viewer engagement. Not my specialty.

I wasn't on Facebook. I didn't tweet. In other words, I didn't exist in the early twenty-first century. I was a modern-day cipher. My old friend Kevin tried to change that. He put me in touch with his older son-in-law, Tony, who owned a house painting business. Tony was a good guy. He hired me to do a bit of social media to get the word out about his company.

I called my younger sister, Kathy, an online marketing guru, to demystify this strange new world for me. I was fearful of pushing the button, so to speak. I didn't want to post a tweet about the paint business and then discover I instead accidentally publicly shared a selfie of the kids and me making silly faces. Not good for the paint business.

But the risk was real, not unlike outfitting a monkey in a spacesuit and then hoping it pulls the right levers and pulleys on the way to outer space. I'm the monkey, by the way. I tried to negotiate against myself. I told Tony I'd help him for free. He didn't have to pay me. I was happy to help out. Heck, he was the son-in-law of a good friend. Tony made an offer of an hourly wage. I thought it was too much. He insisted. I reluctantly agreed.

Fortunately, though, the gig didn't last. Tony didn't need my help. He already had a thriving business. I was relieved when he stopped paying me. It was a good thing I was out of work. The last thing I wanted to be was a burden to Tony or anyone else for that matter. I was already a burden to myself. Especially when I conversed with myself, trying to give myself career advice.

The conversation in my head went something like this: *You're not completely worthless. Yes, I am. Okay. Fine. But you know how to write. You've been helping people with their writing for years. So? So you can do that, start a business offering writing and editing help. All you need is a website— business cards, optional.*

I didn't know where to start. So I started with a name for the firm: Matthew 56 Consulting, LLC. In the Bible, Matthew 5:6 is part of the Gospels where Jesus preached from the mount, teaching his disciples: "Blessed are those who hunger and thirst for righteousness, for they will be filled."

That seemed to capture it all. To me, it didn't matter how "righteousness" was defined. It covered a lot of ground. If you seek goodness, you will find it. If you try to right wrongs, if you try to do the right thing, if you try to lead a better life, if you try to help others, you will be filled. You will be met. It will not be for naught. There will be meaning in it. And the message was inherently eternal. It could apply at anytime, anywhere, to anyone, even me.

I made myself CEO of, well, nothing. Then I offered a

job to my father. It paid nothing—there's that word again—at least for the moment. He could join me in this fiasco of an idea, Matthew 56 Consulting. Only one problem: He didn't like the name.

My father implicitly understood it was a reference to Jesus. He asked whether we could change the company name. I told him I'd already obtained its standing as a limited liability company. I'd already purchased the website. The firm already had a federal tax identification number. And there was this other little factoid I didn't mention: I wasn't changing the name.

Grudgingly, he said he'd give it some thought.

I didn't hear back for some time. I figured he'd dismissed the whole thing. As it turned out, he spent some of that time not talking about it but looking up the biblical reference to Matthew 5:6.

When he called, he reluctantly agreed to go into business with me. I figured, even if the business failed, I at least got my father to read a bit of the Gospels. Another bonus: I decided he deserved top billing: chairman of, well, nothing.

It wasn't without a consideration of the merits. My father had written eleven best sellers to my measly one. Besides, age before beauty, right?

What I didn't appreciate was how my father and I hadn't done anything together since I was a punk of a teenager back in the Cro-Magnon prehistoric age.

Back then, my first writing assignment for the Stuyvesant

High School newspaper, the *Spectator*, was about a mundane burglary of the student union. I put in a modicum of work and showed a draft to my father before submitting it. He scanned it and looked alarmed.

It was the kind of alarm that asked whether we were biologically *related*, that I must have been secretly swapped at birth because there was no other possible explanation for my sheer unadulterated idiocy.

My father asked: "Did you contact a school official?"

"What for?"

"For comment about the burglary."

"No."

"Go do it now."

"How?"

"Pick up the phone book."

"But it's a *school* night."

This was back in the day, pre-internet, when a phone book existed to look up people's numbers. And there she was: Ms. Burman, the school administrator.

After I spoke with Ms. Burman, I dutifully returned to my father, who then asked whether I'd spoken with police about the burglary.

"No."

"Go do it now."

"How?"

"Go down to the police station."

"But I have *homework*."

After I took a subway down to the station and spoke with the police, I dutifully returned to my father, who remained decidedly unsatisfied.

He asked to see my raw notes. Evidently, I did one thing right. I interviewed a school security guard. She told me this was the worst burglary she ever witnessed at the school. Miraculously, I asked her how long she worked at the school, which was something on the order of twenty-four years.

At this point, my father asked me to step aside. Watch the master at work. Hunched at his desk, he refashioned the lead of the story, leaning on the interview with the school security guard, beginning: "In the worst breakout of burglary in nearly a quarter century . . ."

The story ended up on page one, little thanks to me.

The last thing my father and I worked on together was my college application essay. I wrote something trite about my parents' divorce. That quotidian approach alone should have tossed my application in the scrap heap.

Somehow, my father edited that to respectability as I squeaked into a couple of Ivy Leagues, ending up at Brown University, little thanks to me.

Now, flash forward: Here we were so many years later. Two ruined souls. Starting all over. With not much of anything. As it happened, we had other things in common— concepts of writing, how to construct a narrative.

Maybe we could make a go of it. Maybe this would work, the business, Matthew 56 Consulting, LLC. Maybe, after all of these years apart, of the strain of not talking much, we'd get to know each other again. It was another reason to be thankful for my destruction. Had it not been for my fall, I wouldn't have found myself in business with my father. Same for him.

Without his own struggles in the final stages of his life, we wouldn't be here. We certainly wouldn't be chatting about characters moving through space and other theories of writing. It felt a little awkward when I referred to him as "Dad." I wasn't used to it. But I tried. I told him I loved him. He'd tell me he loved me, too. I figured it was a start.

I also figured it wasn't much of a leap to put forth another business idea. Matthew 56 Investigations, LLC. My father had already come part way, joining me in Matthew 56 Consulting.

So why not another one?

Here's where the cockamamie idea came from: an unpublished website. When I abandoned the idea to become a private investigator, I'd got rid of everything. Except the website, Matthew 56 Investigations, the last vestige. I had already paid for it. The website was just sitting there, unpublished.

I'd fiddled with it for some time, constructing it with photos and verbiage. There wasn't anything left to do with the website, other than gaze at it blankly. Until a thought intruded.

Wait. What if. Who said I had to be a private investigator?

Why couldn't I be what I already was? It was like I had been ignoring the elephant in the middle of the room. I was an investigative journalist for a long time. Why couldn't I continue to investigate stuff—things, bad guys, wrongful convictions—using the techniques I was comfortable with, that I knew, that worked for me as an investigative reporter?

It was just a matter of adjusting the lens, in a manner of speaking. It just required a little tweak, a reimagining of the website. Matthew 56 Investigations would be a global—yes, global—investigative firm fashioned after my own experience, based on contemporary investigative journalistic approaches, which is to say, I'd rely on public records and interviews with reliable sources. Everything would be aboveboard.

I bounced the idea off my father, and he liked it so much, he asked: When do we get started? My father was a longtime journalist who had deep experience reporting on politics, the military, and a host of other issues. We were already in it together with Matthew 56 Consulting. It was just another step to Matthew 56 Investigations.

This time, he didn't give me a hard time about the reference to Jesus. He accepted it. He was, for all his reluctance, working under the umbrella of Matthew 5:6: "Blessed are those who hunger and thirst for righteousness, for they will be filled."

Now, we just needed a client.

chapter twelve

When I pull up to the curb at O'Hare International Airport, I have no expectations. I don't even think about the turkey. It will be obtained. Someone will put it in the oven. There will be stuffing. Cranberry will be had. Mere details. More immediate: I can't remember the last time I spent Thanksgiving with my father.

Certainly not in this century.

Things have a way of getting away from us. Okay. Fine. From me. I'm trying to do something about it. That's why I've flown my father here, to Chicago from New York, to spend the holiday together.

I spot him in front of the terminal. He looks tidy, bundled. I'm reminded that once someone tries to commit suicide, there's a higher likelihood it will happen again. He smiles and waves. I smile and wave back. I get out of the car. We hug. It's an okay hug. Slightly stilted. We need practice. Hopefully, there will be time.

Somewhere along the way, I gently remind him my kids don't know what happened to him. They only know he was hospitalized, that he wasn't well, all of which is true. No need to bring up the hundred pills and the plastic bag tied over the head.

When we get to the house, Rosie rushes toward my father until her claws skid to a halt on the hardwood floors. She nearly mauls him.

Welcome to chez Alec.

A homicide is averted. A moment later, we're off again in the car to pick up the kids from school. They pile in, joining my father in the backseat. Rosie is up front, riding shotgun, snuggled on a luxurious furry pillow, wrapped in a stylish blanket.

Hey, there's a pecking order.

My father calls Karen, my older sister, joking that he's been relegated to the backseat. I suspect he's mildly perturbed, scrunched back there, what with his long gangly legs, packed like sardines with the wiggly kids. He'll be up in the passenger seat later.

That happens to be on his first evening in town. I drop him off at a nearby church. No, he hasn't converted yet. He's there for an Alcoholics Anonymous meeting, although I have to say, there seems to be a spiritual dimension to AA from what my father says elliptically about it.

He talks about something called the "Big Book." He talks about the "Twelve Steps," which, by the way, includes believing in a Power greater than ourselves who could restore us. And my father, always the intellectual, notes the origins of AA stem in part from something else called the "Oxford Group," which, as it happens, was a Christian fellowship group founded on the teachings of Jesus in the Sermon on the Mount. That, lest it be overlooked, is where Matthew 5:6 originated.

I tell him I'll pick him up in an hour as he heads to the backdoor of the church, huddled against the wintry wind. A strange sensation comes over me. At first, I'm not sure what it is. Then, as I pull away, it strikes me. A role reversal of sorts. Now it's like I'm the concerned parent and he's the kid I'm dropping off at an activity who'll need a ride home later. I do a lot of this nowadays, chauffeuring the kids. But I don't ever remember my father dropping me off or picking me up in my youth in New York. I took the subway where it was everyone for themselves. But you get the idea. Things come full circle, kind of.

Over the ensuing days, we ride all over town at night, looking for AA meetings squirreled away in churches and synagogue basements. My father goes twice a day when he's in New York. It's so important to him, he's researched meetings for his brief visit here in the Chicago area, scrawling the times and places of AA meetings on a scrap of paper he keeps tucked in his jeans pocket. If I might, there's almost a religious devotion to his attendance at the AA meetings—and to the messages of redemption inherent in them.

And yet, my father's a skeptic. He doesn't believe in an afterlife. I know this because our idea of chitchat is to talk about Jesus. My idea. I have trouble talking about anything else.

He still doesn't approve. Not that he comes right out and says it. But he notes that Jesus was one of many in his time professing to be the Messiah. He brings up, as an example, John the Baptist. Now, hold on. For one, all I do is read about Jesus, so I'm pretty much up to date. And for another, John the Baptist heralded the arrival of the Messiah and baptized Jesus. Big difference.

I let it go. Instead, I talk about the power of Jesus's message—of kindness, of forgiveness, of love. My father doesn't argue with that. I take that as a minor concession. So I offer my own. I admit I still struggle intellectually with the idea of the miracles, of the resurrection. I keep reading books about them because I want to understand the historical basis for such supernatural acts. I want to believe them. But I can't seem to shake my natural skepticism, my journalist's inveterate need for proof.

This much, though, I gather from my voluminous reading: Virtually uncontested by scholars is that Jesus taught great, enduring lessons. He was crucified. He died. Three days later, the tomb where the body was placed was found empty. Subsequently, Jesus's disciples believed they saw the risen Jesus, suffering enormously for that belief over the rest of their lives, ultimately being killed for that belief.

Paul, who had initially persecuted Jesus's followers, said he too saw the risen Jesus after the crucifixion and became perhaps the most influential leader of the early Christian church.

And James, Jesus's brother, a devout Jew known for his virtue, who at first rejected Jesus as the Messiah, also believed he saw the risen Jesus and became a believer and champion of the early church until he was stoned to death for that belief.

Then there's this: Paul said there were more than five hundred people—most still alive when he wrote about it—who also saw the risen Jesus.

Go check it out, Paul was essentially saying. They're still around. They can tell you. Would Paul risk saying that, were it not true? Even if one of those five hundred plus denied seeing the risen Jesus, it could have threatened the just-emerging church Paul so fervently sought to build in the face of constant persecution, beatings, and imprisonment.

So, what's wrong with me? Why can't I just say, yeah, okay, I accept everything; that's enough for me?

I don't reveal all these doubts to my father, but I do confess I have doubts, and in the process, I begin to feel like Peter.

First of the twelve apostles, Peter disavowed Jesus three times before the crucifixion. I've been tough on Peter, if I'm allowed to say that. I passed judgment on his lack of courage in the moment—at the critical moment—even if Peter made up for it during the rest of his life, spreading the Gospel, ultimately paying the ultimate price. Indeed, Peter felt so unworthy of being crucified as Jesus was put to death, Peter asked to be crucified upside down.

But now I kind of get it. I can see where Peter was coming from. In the moment, you might hesitate, you might doubt. What's more, who am I to judge Peter, only one of the greatest figures of Christianity? Or to paraphrase Jesus, "Let he who is without sin cast the first stone."

My father suggests I read a popular book, *Zealot*, that offers a different view of Jesus. I order it and find myself immediately dubious as the author notes upfront there are few historical records about Jesus, little more than the Gospels, so he'll have to make some educated guesses. Wait. Hold on. Did that author just say he'd guess? Isn't that like saying his is a book of fiction?

I'm worried. Not just about the fiction. I'm worried because I can see where this is headed, a dismantling of Jesus, which it is.

But in the dismantling, even that author remarkably

can't account for one major historical fact backed by documentation: Jesus was famous for performing miracles—restoring sight to the blind, bringing back hearing to the deaf, healing the sick, raising the dead—that word quickly spread throughout Capernaum and the surrounding seaside environs of first-century Israel, drawing huge crowds wherever Jesus preached. Indeed, the author of the book, who seeks to strip Jesus of divinity, cannot explain away these miracles. That author tries, noting other contemporaries of Jesus were known for their healing powers, but they usually charged people for those healings. Not Jesus. Jesus freely healed all, which drew even more masses to witness the miracles, to experience them firsthand. There was no endgame. Even those who sought to discredit Jesus in the early centuries after the crucifixion did not challenge the idea Jesus was well known for performing great miracles. Those early critics of the church tried to dismiss those miracles of Jesus as mere acts of magic, or sorcery.

But the great unexplainable acts of healing that Jesus performed stood then and now, even among the greatest of the skeptics and scholars.

So, in a strange way, a book meant to ostensibly cast doubt on my growing faith actually reinforced it. I read all the books I could get my hands on—and I continue to grasp for them—but in the end, they can't offer the proof I want. Instead, I choose to believe. I choose to believe the miracles. I choose to believe the resurrection. For me, it's a leap of faith, it's an act of devotion, as is my public declaration soon after, when I'm submerged in a kiddie pool and baptized.

There's also an element of the rational. When I pray, it is to God and Jesus, one and the same. And I can't be praying to God without the resurrection. Thus, God must've risen. It wouldn't be much of a stretch for God to come back from the dead, anyway. Creating the universe seems a bit more arduous, at least from my limited vantage. Could you imagine how complicated it was to invent the idea of, say, a tree? I'm amazed by lesser mortal phenomenon, including how Shazam, an app on my iPhone, can basically identify any tune in a matter of seconds.

Then there's this: The alternative, that Jesus didn't rise from the dead, would require a rather vast conspiracy of lies and obfuscation that defies logic. It would require the stealing away of his body. It would call for the women who found the empty cave to be lying. It would necessitate that Paul falsified his encounter with Jesus after the crucifixion and willingly went to his own grave for it. It would mean that more than 500 witnesses to the risen Jesus were mistaken. It would mean Jesus's brother, James, died a horrible death for no reason. It would mean Peter suffered and perished for nothing. All of which is to say, the alternative makes no sense. It needs too much in the way of unrealistic contortions. As hard as it is to conceive of the supernatural, it is the only thing that is natural.

How else can I explain the presence of Christ wherever

I go? I feel God in the people I keep encountering: the mechanic and the barber who, though far flung from each other, each speaks Aramaic, the native language Jesus taught the world; and a new friend, the son of two pastors who witnessed a miracle, a parent riddled with tumors suddenly cured of them all. I recognize the presence of God in the stories I watch on TV, where the hero sacrifices herself, substituting for another, in an act of selfless love. I notice God where I didn't before, when I pass by, slumped in the backseat of an Uber, the corner of 119th Street and First Avenue in the heart of Harlem, site of a shack of a church built on Christ. Now it makes sense when I think of Mariano Rivera, the great Yankee closer and believer, famed for nothing less than saves. My workspace at home is surrounded by Jesus: a pocketbook of the Gospels, a magazine cover that tells "The Story of Jesus," a printout of a painted portrait of Jesus standing by the seashore, surrounded by his disciples. When I talk about God, I have to be careful because I can suddenly find myself on the verge of unexpected emotion. I can't explain it. It can't be helped. It's what's in my heart.

Not that I won't keep asking questions. It's how I'm built. Among the questions: I asked my father whether he would read the book I sent him, *The Case for Christ*. There was silence. I pressed. He offered a terse yes. Why was I trying to proselytize?

As it happened, I didn't need to. My father was on his own path of discovery, whether he admitted it or not. His

devotion to AA—historically based on Jesus's teachings—
was such an integral part of his life he adhered to its precepts,
particularly the idea of making amends, another concept of
Christ, of restoration, of redemption.

That's why we were sitting at my kitchen table, my
father and me. It was part of the Twelve Steps. He wanted
to make amends. To apologize. He said he was sorry for
what he did, for my childhood, when he took my sister and
me away from our mother, for how he treated my mother
all those years ago.

He said he had been angry. He said he was afraid after
what happened to me as a child, when I was five years old,
when I was molested. He didn't remember the man's name. I
did. For years, I wouldn't eat Ritz crackers because I remembered the molester liked them. I eat Ritz crackers now. Not
just because they're pretty darn tasty. But just because. I'm
not going to let a molester decide anything for me.

I forgive you, I told my father.

Jesus came up again. I couldn't help myself. I explained
my journey to faith. How I read the Gospels. What I discovered from the teachings of Jesus. About forgiveness. About
not judging others.

My little speech about Jesus almost ruined my father's
apology. He seemed uncomfortable. But this, for him, was
part of the process, the Twelve Steps. He'd already made
amends with my Japanese mother. He apologized to her
for taking away her children, for leaving her with nothing.

The grace she showed in response was in broken but beautiful English: "You asked me if any or one thing you can do for me . . . so I like you to promise me one thing if again slightest feeling of desperation visit you, please call me or anyone . . . you are going through the changes which is hard. . . . I experienced myself so many times . . . so I know . . . but you have very caring family including me . . . ask us help . . . you asked me if anything you can do for me . . . thinking about . . . and this my utmost wish! Would you grant this for me?"

Now, every so often, they have tea together. My mother says he looks great. He says she hasn't aged a day. Oh, boy. I don't want to know anything more. But it's good. They've made amends. I have, too. I didn't need to say the words, but Julie-Ann has forgiven me. She didn't need to say the words either. I could just feel it. The anger from our years of marriage has vanished—just like that—a veritable snap of the fingers. This feels like a miracle to me.

I start to feel like maybe there are miracles all around us, if we just take notice, if we just acknowledge the remarkable things happening around us that we take for granted. We dismiss so much as happenstance, as sheer luck, as a random confluence of unnecessary factors. My son, for one. He's a miracle. During Julie-Ann's pregnancy, she woke up in a pool of blood. After a bunch of diagnostic tests, the doctor told us there was no chance for our unborn child, though there was still a faint heartbeat. The doctor shook my hand

and offered his condolences. Reeling from the prognosis, I was dispatched to fetch a prescription for Julie-Ann, a pain-killer to ease her suffering when the fetus would inevitably be expelled. I'll never forget the drive to the pharmacy. A sudden torrential downpour blinded my windshield. I almost didn't make it. But after I returned home with the pills, I told Julie-Ann she should take the painkillers if she needed them. But could she hold off until then? The heavy dosage of medication alone would end all hope, and despite what the doctor pronounced, I still believed there was hope. When there is a heartbeat, there is hope.

Julie-Ann never took the painkiller. Years later, the miracle lives, our son. (Our daughter is a miracle, too, in the name of fairness.)

Julie-Ann, for her part, has forgiven me for the hurt of our neglected marriage from years gone by. She's openly wept because of my suffering now. She's become one of my fiercest defenders. Turns out, she's a lot tougher than I am.

I always thought I was pretty tough. I run this idea by my older sister Karen. She was always the wise one in the family. Wasn't I tough? I ask Karen. No, she says instantly. So, what are you saying, I was a wuss? Yes, she says instantly.

Karen has that humorless tone in her voice, as if to say: Can you ask me a more serious question because this one is so obvious, it doesn't deserve more than a monosyllabic answer? She also has the kindness not to remind me of our childhood when she nicknamed me "SS." Super Sensitive.

Fine. Okay. But the point is, Julie-Ann has so thoroughly forgiven me, she's cooking up a storm for Thanksgiving. She has a giant bird in the oven. She's whipped up gourmet stuffing, mashed potatoes, gravy, and three pies, two courtesy of our daughter, a baking maven. When we assemble at the table, with my father invited to sit at the head and the kids digging into the food, it feels like a family.

It *is* a family. Not a perfect family. Eons from it. But Julie-Ann and I, we're friends. She says she'll always support me unless I do something really bad. She's half kidding. I tell her I'll always support her even if she does something really bad. I'm not kidding.

She is, after all, the mother of my children. We're talking about a family road trip in the minivan to New York to see my family for Christmas. Rosie would come along. Wouldn't leave without her. She's family.

Before my father leaves after Thanksgiving, I hand him a little box. It contains two sets of business cards with his name on them. On one set, the Matthew 56 Consulting business card, it reads: "Chairman." On the other set of cards, Matthew 56 Investigations: "Senior Partner." Same as me.

At O'Hare, we hug. Still needs some work. But I'll see him again soon. We can practice then. I ask him to text me when he arrives home in New York, so I know he's okay. There's that thing again. Role reversal.

Back at the house, remnants of Oklahoma follow me. I still hear from my friends. I find myself still helping inmates there and elsewhere. I still speak with Amber once a week from prison. We're going over her written remarks to the parole board—again and again—seeking to commute her life sentence after failing drug court. I don't care about grammar, misspellings, or punctuation. What I care about is the sentiment in every word. Every word must be authentic. Every word is precious. Every word, I hope, will lead Amber one step closer to freedom on the eve of her appearance before the Oklahoma parole board:

> I would like to thank you for this opportunity to speak. First I would like to tell you I have 2 years 6 months clean and for the first time I'm excited for my future. Since I've been here I've taken many classes but one really stuck out to me and that is Victim's Impact. I use to always think I wasn't hurting anyone but myself, but now I know I hurt everyone around me and others I didn't know. I just want to say I'm truely [sic] sorry for committing these crimes and sorry for hurting everyone. I know I can't go back and change anything but what I do know is I can start by taking Responsibility [sic] for my actions, then I can be a productive citizen in the community and give back. I can also be a good mother, daughter and friend. I really want you to know I value this opportunity to stand before you. I'm ready to be released from prison and be reunited with my family. I

look forward to be [sic] a good parent to my 3 wonderful children. I love my kids and I want to be a good role model for them. I want you to know I have made plans for my release because failure is not an option for me. I plan to live at Rhonda Bears [sic] transitional home. I have a job at she brews [sic]. I plan to attend support meetings, And [sic] I plan to continue working with dogs like I have been doing in the Guardian Angels program. These are just some of the plans I have. I read my devotional and pray daily for healing and to be reunited with my children and family and I pray that the women on this yard find peace and healing. I truely [sic] want to thank you for considering commuting my sentence. I would like to thank my family and friends for being here today to support me. If you give me this chance I will not let you down. Thank you from the bottom of my heart.

Meanwhile, I too continue to pray daily and read about God. I'm ordering books left and right, and my friend Stacie, bless her heart, sends me a steady stream of books about faith—*Peace Is a Lifestyle, God's Big Picture,* and more.

Mine isn't a perfect faith. Not nearly. It's still evolving. It's still finding me. I'm still finding me. I'm not the same, though. I'm not the man I was. The change is inside me, emanating from within. I'm told that even amidst the doubts, even if I'm seeking answers, I'm seeking God, which is a good thing.

I hope that's true. Because I know this isn't a fairy tale with a happy ending. I know there will be more suffering ahead. I know this because I have no idea how I'm going to support my children, my family. Julie-Ann is doing her best, working long hours, but her new sales job is a tough racket. I don't know how much more time we have before we lose the house. I have a single client. My father and I are rediscovering our relationship; turns out, we work well together. He writes, I edit. I write, he edits. When it comes to the craft of writing, we often think alike. It's seamless, almost effortless. We talk on the phone nearly every day. "Love you, Dad." "Love you, too." It almost feels natural—the tie between the son and the father. Even more natural is my renewed relationship with my son and daughter—the children and the father. And then there is my connection to the ultimate father, God. It's a trinity of fathers.

And yet I can't see a clearing, a path forward. I know the rebuild, if there is a rebuild, is a long way off. Even the elders of a church I consider joining are worried about blowback for associating with me. And some things are gone for good. That includes The Medill Justice Project, which the school shut down about a year after my resignation. What could I do? I just hope no one else but I will have to suffer for the destruction, that Julie-Ann and the kids will be all right, no matter what happens to me. Because I'm getting used to the suffering. I can almost embrace it. Heck, we live together. Constant companions, suffering and me. We're practically friends, if suffering wasn't so ornery, so unforgiving.

I'm still trying to figure things out. I still don't like leaving the house. I still don't shave much. I still live a life of quiet despair even as I feel a greater sense of peace. I know, a contradiction. I can't explain it. I just accept. I continue to pray. I continue to pray for forgiveness. I continue to pray to forgive. I continue to pray that I am grateful. I wouldn't have found my way to faith—even as I wrestle with it—without the bone-crushing suffering. I was too stubborn, too set in my ways, too comfortable, too much a creature of habit, too much of me. I needed a good swift kick in the pants. It's brought me closer to my faith, to God. So, thank you.

Every day, I pray with the kids. Kneeling, my daughter prays to play well in her next basketball game. My son prays for another snow day off from school. They both pray for Rosie's good health and long life.

I pray for kindness. There's so much anger and hatred and cruelty in the world, it feels like it's going to implode from spontaneous combustion, from all the raging vitriol on the internet, from the vicious, impromptu, knee-jerk comments on Twitter, from the anonymous attacks on the web, the public shamings, the false accusations and the online stonings, all of the evils of this hard-edged digital age.

Children already have this figured out. They already belong to the Kingdom, as Jesus said. They see the light. The adults need a bit of work. I'm sure of this because recently I was standing in the hallway of my son's elementary school, waiting to attend a recital in his music class, when I couldn't help but marvel at what I saw.

There, in the school hallway, posted on the wall, were self-portraits drawn by the children, each with a word bubble expressing their wishes:

"I think everyone should be nice!"

"I wish the world could be in peace!"

"I wish nobody was homeless."

"I want pore [sic] people to have money."

"I want to make the world a better place!"

"I wish that people were nicer to animals!"

"I wish I could play professional hockey."

Okay. Fine. It wasn't unanimous. But pretty close.

The problem isn't the internet. It isn't Twitter's fault. We can't legislate kindness. We can't enforce forgiveness. We can't cut the weed, as the saying goes, and expect to fix the problem. We need to pull out the root. To get to the cause. To get to what Jesus was saying all those years ago that applied then and applies today and tomorrow and forever.

I'm still a work in progress, by the way. I was reminded of this recently when I had to call Verizon about my erroneous phone bill. I couldn't reach a human being. I had to call multiple times, trapped in the vortex, the dark hole of the automated system, forced to answer a series of questions that fell just short of standing on one leg, touching the tip of my nose with both index fingers while singing the national anthem. I lost my cool. Not cool. By the time I reached a customer service representative, I was chaste. Slightly exhausted. A little bummed out. I was speaking in a quiet voice. I failed myself. I let the automated system get the better of me, disrupting my sense of peace.

So I keep at it. I keep working on it, on a deeper sense of faith. In the gloaming, I see a spider dangling in the bathroom. Threatened, I'm about to smash it. Then hesitate. It wants to live, too. It is one of God's creatures. I let it be. See ya later. Don't bring friends. It goes about its business.

As for me, I'm still pondering the miracles. On a recent morning, I received a text from my friend, Rhonda: "It's a unanimous yes, Amber has made it." I could hardly believe it. The parole board did it. The members voted to set Amber free, leaving only the governor's signature to make it a reality.

Moments later, Amber called me from prison, feeling overwhelmed, having wept. "I'm on, like, cloud nine," she said, thanking me for helping her. I felt like weeping, too. I told her it was my honor to help. Within days, the governor signed the commutation papers. About three years into a life sentence after failing drug court, Amber was finally going home, to be with her children in time for Christmas. Now that was a miracle, I'd have to admit.

Another miracle: The parole board approved Robyn Allen's commutation. Same for Sheila Royal.

The thing was, in the year of my public disgrace, of

the utter dismantling of my life, when I didn't want to live anymore, I was able to help more prisoners than ever. Three of those inmates, one wrongfully convicted and two others excessively sentenced, were set free from life in prison—in the span of months. Dozens of women, excessively sentenced, were freed on parole based on a system that would help immeasurably more. All of that, I reckon, was miraculous.

Meanwhile, I continued my feverish reading, including a book recommended in passing by my good friend, Stacie. A novel called *The Harbinger*, I promptly ordered it and found myself immediately struck by a truth within it: We've lost our way. As a society, we've moved away from God. We've become a den of skeptics and cynics who cordon off faith, who dismiss God from our public lives, from our interior lives.

I'm struck by another truth: the power of the word. There's a role for the writer. Especially now. In a time of such enormous negativity, filled with venom, a hardness of the heart, marked by a lack of faith, a separation from God. Writing, as it happens, is one of the only things I know how to do.

When I complete this memoir, literary agents say they are afraid of representing me, even though they haven't read my story; they say they would be blackballed for simply trying to find a publisher for me. That's the world of fear we inhabit today. The marketplace of ideas has been constricted by the terror of attacks online, and freedom of speech isn't so free anymore. So I find a publisher on my own. But those who had attacked me nearly two years earlier get wind of the book's impending release. They intimidate the publisher, and the distributor suddenly declines to distribute the memoir before publication. The publisher promptly kills the book.

I think it's over. I accept God's will. But then, in a matter of days, another publisher materializes, and here we are, resurrected. I consider it a miracle. And it occurs to me, maybe there's a reason. In the aftermath, just maybe, there's a use for the writer, for the word. A calling. Of the need for kindness, for forgiveness, for another way.